W9-AON-205

DOWN & DIRTY

DOWN & DIRTY!

43 Fun & Funky First-Time Projects & Activities to Get You Gardening

For Paul & Ceci, with love, Ellen

Ellen Zachos

Photography by ADAM MASTOON

Storey Publishing

*The mission of Storey Publishing is to serve our customers by publishing practical information
that encourages personal independence in harmony with the environment.*

Edited by Gwen Steege
Cover design by Kent Lew
Interior design and layout by Vicky Vaughn
Interior layout and production by Liseann Karandisecky
Cover and interior photographs © by Adam Mastoon
Additional interior photographs credited on page 239
Illustrations by Brigita Fuhrmann
Indexed by Sunday Oliver

© 2007 by Ellen Zachos

All rights reserved. No part of this book may be reproduced without written permission from the publisher, except
by a reviewer who may quote brief passages or reproduce illustrations in a review with appropriate credits; nor
may any part of this book be reproduced, stored in a retrieval system, or transmitted in any form or by any means
— electronic, mechanical, photocopying, recording, or other — without written permission from the publisher.

The information in this book is true and complete to the best of our knowledge. All recommendations are made
without guarantee on the part of the author or Storey Publishing. The author and publisher disclaim any liability
in connection with the use of this information. For additional information please contact Storey Publishing, 210
MASS MoCA Way, North Adams, MA 01247.

Storey books are available for special premium and promotional uses and for customized editions. For further
information, please call 1-800-793-9396.

Printed in the China by Elegance
10 9 8 7 6 5 4 3 2 1

LIBRARY OF CONGRESS CATALOGING-IN-PUBLICATION DATA

Zachos, Ellen.
    Down & dirty : 43 fun & funky first-time projects & activities to get you gardening / Ellen Zachos ;
photography by Adam Mastoon.
        p. cm.
    Includes bibliographical references and index.
    ISBN 13: 978-1-58017-641-5; ISBN 10: 1-58017-641-0 (pbk. : alk. paper)
    ISBN 13: 978-1-58017-642-2; ISBN 10: 1-58017-642-9 (hardcover : alk. paper)
    1. Gardening. I. Title. II. Title: Down and dirty.
SB453.Z27 2007
635—dc22
                                                                        2006023059

Dedication

To John Keane, who has been my most demanding editor since college. His discerning criticism and suggestions make me a better writer. But while I depend upon his editorial skills and encyclopedic knowledge, I would never *dream* of holding him responsible for any factual errors, which are most certainly my fault alone.

Acknowledgments

I am eternally grateful to my husband, Michael, for his patience, understanding, and support. (And this time he actually let us use his picture!) Also thanks to Gwen Steege, for inspiration, friendship, and the loan of her garden; to Adam Mastoon for superb photographs, humor, and infinite tact; and to Vicky Vaughn for creative vision, insight, and letting us use her brand-new home. It's been great fun being part of this team. Finally, thanks to the friends, family, and total strangers who lent themselves to this project. I'll enjoy looking at your faces and remembering your personalities for years to come.

Finding Your Place in the Gardening World

DOWN & DIRTY PROJECTS
Accent your outdoor space and try out your new skills

DOWN & DIRTY PLANTS
Find out how cool plants really are

LOOKING FOR MORE FUN IDEAS?

Recipes
Liven up your menu with foods from your garden . . . and beyond

Container Gardens
Discover the art of gardening in small spaces

Kids and Families
It's never too early to begin

Welcome to My World!

My own mother never taught me how to garden. She tried, but in my formative years the sight of an earthworm sent me screaming, so my yard chores were limited to mowing the lawn and picking up after the dog, which stimulated my gag reflex, but didn't give me nightmares. My father's mother was a legendary gardener, in the way Greek peasant women often are. My *yiayia* could grow anything — fruits, vegetables, flowers. She died when I was eight, long before I conquered my fear of earthworms or learned to speak Greek.

So how did I end up as a professional gardener? It's the kind of job that makes people stop and ask, "Can you make a *living* doing that?" Some days I can't believe it either, and I know I have the best job in the world. Catch me one morning in May when the breeze is fresh, the sun is bright, and I'm alone with my pruning shears and some overgrown shrubbery. That's my idea of heaven.

Gardening feeds the heart, mind, and body. It's an avocation, it's a vocation, it's a passion, it's a duty, it's hard work, it's creative indulgence. Gardening gives you perspective and optimism. If you don't think the sun will come up tomorrow, what's the point of planting a seed?

Most people look at gardening as a mysterious skill, something you're born with, an innate ability. But guess what? There is no gardening gene. It's not encoded in your DNA. This is an acquired skill, people. It's never too late to start, and no space is too small for a garden.

I was a late bloomer myself. My horticultural skills lay dormant until I was given a houseplant as an opening-night gift — a lifetime ago, when I was on the Broadway stage. The days are long gone when you work for one company, do one thing, have one job, your whole life. I'm on my second adventure: my first career was in musical theatre. I did *Les Miz* on Broadway and toured the country in roles as diverse as Maria Von Trapp and Mary Magdalene. It was while I was doing *Fiddler on the Roof* that the gift of a peace lily got me hooked on plants. The love of gardening snuck up on me; as I became more involved in making things grow, I became less willing to tour with *Cats*. (I could have been the opera cat!)

One passion replaced another, and I hung up my dancing shoes. (Not really . . . they're in the attic.) Now I garden professionally in New York City four days a week and for myself (and Michael and the *real* cats) in Pennsylvania the other three. It might seem odd to someone who drives to the same office every day, but for me, for now, it's just right. And since it was far too late to learn at my mother's (or *yiayia's*) knee, I read, I took classes, I pestered everyone I could with questions. And I learned. So can you.

I know it's daunting to look at your yard and have no idea where to start. The pressure of having to come up with a concept, a design, a 5-year plan, can be overwhelming. So don't do it. Start with *one* thing. Anybody can do one thing, right? Think of the millions of people out there who've planted one thing. Could they all be smarter, better, and more talented than you? Of course not.

Look through the table of contents and pick a project (one thing) that speaks to you, and start there. If you succeed (and if you honestly try, you *will* succeed), you'll understand the rush that comes from making things grow. Then, if I have my way, you'll pick another project: one *more* thing.

The idea is to learn by doing. Each project teaches a skill. Some projects build on skills taught through a project somewhere else in the book, in which case I'll refer you to that technique. Some skills are used over and over again, because a little practice never hurts. If you do every project in this book, you'll know almost as much as I do.

I want you to love gardening, and since nothing motivates like success, I've written *Down & Dirty* to make it as easy as possible for you to succeed. This book won't tell you everything you'll ever need to know about gardening. It *will* get you started and then some, encouraging you to dig in, and get down and dirty in the garden.

Now, take a look at that table of contents and pick a project — personally I suggest Container Gardening au Naturel. And welcome to my world!

Forcing Spring Bulbs

1

Nothing says spring is on the way like snowdrops pushing up through the mulch in Central Park. Or in your own backyard, for that matter. Early-spring bulbs are harbingers of warmth and light, a much cheerier symbol of rebirth than biting the head off a chocolate bunny.

Whether you have a yard, a deck, a window box, or no outdoor space whatsoever, you can jump-start spring by forcing bulbs indoors. It's a simple process, and can be done on any scale. All you need is a cool, dark place, where the temperature is between 35° and

Tulip treatment. If you're forcing tulips, you'll notice one side of the bulb is flattened (not the bottom). Face this side toward the outside of the pot. This is where the first, large leaf will come from. The display looks best when the large leaf leans out over the edge of the pot, creating a full circumference of foliage.

Hyacinth hint. If you notice your hyacinth bloom is short and clasped between the leaves, make a little paper cone and place it over the flower. Keeping the flower in the dark will slow its development while the stalk lengthens.

45°F. This could be a garage, an unheated cellar, under a porch, in a cold frame, or in the vegetable drawer of the refrigerator.

Get yourself a minimum-maximum thermometer at a hardware store (about $10) and place it where you think the bulbs should be chilled. Check the range over a week, and if the temp is right, gather your supplies. You'll need bulbs, potting mix, pots, and pottery shards. The type and size (of everything) will depend on what you like and how much space you have. (see How to Force Tulips on facing page.) You can find bulbs for forcing at local garden centers and home stores, but if you want to experiment with more unusual, hard-to-find beauties, why not mail order? You can view catalogs online or request a hard copy by telephone or snail mail (see appendix).

Are you in a tiny studio apartment with a fire escape facing a dark courtyard? Brighten up your winter landscape with a series of small bulbs in matching pots or baskets. Pot up miniature daffodils, crocuses, species tulips, and grape hyacinths singly in 4-inch pots to create a horticultural lineup.

After They Bloom

After your forced bulbs have bloomed, move the pot outdoors (if possible) and keep it watered until the foliage turns yellow and wilts. Then plant the bulbs in the garden to carry them over to next year, but don't try to force them again. Bulbs that have been forced are weak and may need an extra year before they rebloom.

A Built-In Food Supply

Each bulb already contains all the nutrition it requires to bloom. In fact, a bulb is almost *pure* nutrition. Bulbs are modified leaf tissue that store food produced by the foliage during the growing season. By the end of the season the flower for the coming spring is already formed inside.

Force Tulips

If you have the space, fill a larger pot (or three) with lots of bigger bulbs: hybrid tulips, daffodils, and hyacinths. Different bulbs grow at different rates, so to have a pot full of uniform bloom, plant one type of bulb per pot.

Once your bulbs are placed, fill in around them with potting mix, leaving about a ½ inch of space between the soil surface and the pot rim. Water well and store in the "cold" place. Don't let it get too cold; not all bulbs tolerate freezing temps. If the cold spot isn't dark, place the pot(s) in a dark trash bag to block light. Check the pot every week; if it feels dry, water it.

preparing the pot

Choose a clay or a plastic pot. Set a pottery shard over the hole in the pot to keep soil from dribbling out the bottom. (If the pot doesn't have a drainage hole, don't use it.) Add soil to the pot. Potted bulbs should be planted twice as deep as they are tall, so gauge accordingly. Measure from the top of the bulb, so that a 2" bulb is covered by 4" of soil. Plastic will keep the potting mix moister longer, but isn't beautiful. When you bring it inside, slip a plastic pot into a cachepot. (French for "hide-pot," cachepot is a term used to describe a pretty container used to cover a not-so-pretty container.)

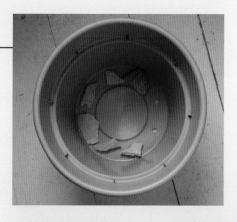

right side up

Place the bulbs in the pot, pointy end up; roots will grow from the flat end. If you're using a large pot, position the bulbs as close together as you can, without allowing them to touch each other or the edge of the pot. The number of bulbs you can fit will depend on the size of the bulb (tulip = large, scilla = small, for example) and the size of the pot.

Different bulbs need to chill for different lengths of time. When they're ready, you'll see fine roots coming out the drainage hole of the pot, and an inch or two of green leaves sprouting from the top of the bulb.

Keep the bulbs between 50° and 60°F for the first week, if you can; this gives the foliage a head start on the flowers. After that, if you keep the bulbs on the cool side, the flowers will last longer.

Bulb	Chilling time
Crocus	14 weeks
Grape hyacinth	14 weeks
Daffodil	15 weeks
Scilla	13 weeks
Tulip	15 weeks
Hyacinth	11 weeks

Pampered Paperwhites

Not all bulbs need to be chilled before flowering. Paperwhite narcissus (*Narcissus* is the botanical name for daffodil) and amaryllis can both be forced without a cold spell. Plant them as you would bulbs you are chilling, or place the bulbs in a nonporous vase or bowl. Surround the bulbs with small stones to hold them in place, then pour water onto the stones, leaving the pointy nose of the bulb just above the stones (and water). Top off the water whenever it gets low; developing roots must be kept constantly wet. Paperwhites have a *very* strong smell; you either love it or you hate it.

Paperwhites are especially easy to force indoors.

Plant Bulbs Directly in the Ground

If "forcing" bulbs sounds too aggressive, try planting some in the ground. The best time to do this (for spring bloomers) is in fall — before the earth has frozen, but when you can still see the placement of your perennials. It's discouraging to dig a bulb hole and unintentionally cut into the roots of a valued plant.

Bulbs planted in the garden should be buried three times as deep as they are tall. The truth is that they have contractile roots and can gradually adjust their own planting depth in case you're a little bit off, but try to get it right the first time. I gravitate toward the little bulbs, since digging 2 inches in my rocky soil is a lot easier than digging the 6 inches required for some of the jumbo narcissus bulbs.

Bulb foliage should be left to yellow on the plant (storing as much energy as possible inside the bulb for next year's flowers), so don't mow the lawn within a naturalized bulb planting until the foliage has faded. You shouldn't braid the foliage or loop it neatly with elastic bands. The leaf surface needs to be exposed to the sun in order to photosynthesize, so you're just going to have to tolerate a little natural messiness in the lawn or garden.

tuck them in

For a naturalized effect, scatter a handful of bulbs on the lawn and plant them where they land. Use a trowel to dig a small hole three times as deep as the height of the bulb.

Plant a Seed, grow a Garden

I am not a patient woman. Ask anyone. (Let's go, I don't have all day.) But watching seeds germinate is such a fascinating process that even I, for whom the words *hurry up* have an almost magical quality, enjoy every minute of it. And I can think of at least three really good reasons to start plants from seed:

1. The feeling of accomplishment is enormous. There's nothing like looking at a plant in your garden and saying, "I made this!"

2. It's way cheaper to buy seeds than to buy plants. A package of seeds usually costs less than $2 and that's for 10 to 30 seeds.

3. Some unusual plants are difficult to find, but their seeds are more readily available.

Shiso Perilla
Red (Akashiso)
Perilla frutescens 'crispa'

$1.79
Net Weight
750 mg

Annual
Warm season
crop - plant after
last chance of
spring frost

*Love basil? Try
Shiso - it is an
intoxicating,
flavorful herb
that should be
as popular as
basil or cilantro!
Also an attrac-
tive bedding
plant!*

Botanical Interests ™

Damping-Off

Damping-off disease is a heart breaker. Your seeds have germinated, their brave little stems reaching upward, one or two leaves soaking up the sun. You feel swell. The next day you check your seedlings again, anticipating the rush of pride that accompanies successful germination. But wait! Can it be? What evil lurks in the seedling flat? Where yesterday there were young, healthy seedlings, today there are dead, wilted, collapsed remnants of plants that will never bear fruit (or flowers or anything at all). *This* is damping-off disease.

DOD is a catchall term for seedling plant death usually caused by fungi. Fungi living in the soil penetrate soft, young stem tissue, which becomes shrunken and discolored. The stem can no longer support itself and it collapses and falls over. Death is inevitable and swift.

Seed starting is a low-tech, inexpensive operation. Although there are plenty of cool gadgets, you really need only a few basics: a lightweight seed-starting mix, a few flats or large shallow pots, some biodegradable pots made of peat or newsprint, and seeds.

Potting mix. You *do* need a special potting mix to start the seeds. Garden soil is heavy and retains so much moisture that seeds may rot. Also, it probably contains soil pathogens like the fungi that cause damping-off disease (see at left). It's sad to watch seedlings poke up all fresh and green, only to come back the next day and find them rotten, brown, and mushy. Save yourself the heartache; use a special seed-starting mix and don't overwater. This will keep seeds moist but not wet and help keep fungi at bay.

Planting flat. A *flat* is a rectangular pan with drainage holes in the bottom that is used for starting lots of seeds at once. It's usually 2 or 3 inches deep. Start one kind of seed per flat, because different seeds have different needs and all the seeds in a single flat or pot will get the same kind of care. If you don't have a flat, use a large, shallow flower pot. Plastic pots are handier than clay because they retain moisture longer and thus require less frequent watering. If the delicate roots of seedlings dry out, they're toast.

Individual pots. Some plants (such as morning glories) are finicky about being transplanted; they don't like having their roots disturbed. Start these in individual biodegradable pots, made of peat or newspaper. When seedlings are ready, you can plant the entire pot in the garden with no root disturbance.

The seeds. Read the seed packets before getting started. Seeds vary in the time, planting depth, and light they require for germination.

Germinating Germplasm

Most seeds germinate more quickly with bottom heat. For this, try a heat mat. Use a special, waterproof heating mat, *not* a regular heating pad. If this isn't an option, try putting the flat on top of the refrigerator, which is usually one of the warmest spots in the house. Unfortunately, though, the light there probably isn't great.

Use row markers to label your seed-starting flats and keep the potting mix moist.

A cool tool you might want to consider is an all-inclusive seed-starting setup that includes a heat mat, insulating base, and clear plastic cover. I'm not telling you to run out and buy one right away, but if you discover you love starting seeds, it's an excellent device.

Let There Be Light

Place the flats (or pots) on your sunniest windowsill. Most of us don't have large expanses of uninterrupted sunny windowsill, of course, so here's where fluorescent lights come in handy. Place your seed flats under fluorescent tubes, with the lights about 4 inches away from the soil surface. As the seeds grow, you'll raise the lights (or lower the seed flats), maintaining a 4-inch difference. Without adequate light, your seedlings will be spindly. (Interested? See Keep Your Distance, page 200.) Remember, heat and light dry out the potting mix, so you'll have to water more frequently.

Watering Rules

Seed packets indicate how long the seeds take to germinate. During this germination period, it's important to keep the potting mix moist but not wet, and high humidity is also helpful. Check the surface of the potting mix every day; if it feels dry to the touch, water. You don't want to disturb seed placement, so water from the bottom, as you did when you first planted the seeds (see page 15). Once the seedlings have sprouted, you can water from above, but be gentle. Break the force of the water by pouring it through your fingers or by using a rose attached to your watering can.

(Interested? See Keep Your Distance, page 200.)

A Rose by Any Other Name

Why do they call the spout on the end of the watering can a rose? It doesn't look like a rose. It doesn't smell like a rose. And yet, it's called a rose. This is the round endpiece, with numerous small holes, that screws onto the end of some watering cans. Pouring water through it creates a delicate sprinkling effect, perfect for delivering a gentle flow of water that won't disturb seeds or seedlings. But here's the thing: screw it on so the holes are facing upward! The pressure of the water from the can will create a fountain effect, pushing water up and out.

cotyledon

Cotyledons are the pair of small round leaves near the soil. The leaves above those are "true leaves."

Direct Sowing

Some seeds are best sown directly in the garden bed. Maybe you want one of those plants that are fussy about transplanting, or the seed requires cold temperatures to get started. Check out the seed packet; it should tell you if you have one that needs special handling.

Prepare the garden soil by making sure it's fluffy, smooth, and nutritious (see It Ain't Just Dirt, page 216), then follow the package instructions regarding sowing depth and spacing. Protect newly sown seeds from voracious marauding birds by covering them (the seedlings, not the birds) with a piece of chicken wire or screen.

A Plant Is Born

The first leaf to emerge is called the *cotyledon*, which means seed leaf. (Some plants produce a pair of cotyledons.) This is not a true leaf; it was originally contained inside the seed case as a source of nutrition for the seedling. The next leaves to emerge will be *true leaves*. All cotyledons are rounded and green — never shaped or variegated, as are many plants' true leaves.

If your germination success rate is high, you'll need to thin the seedlings before transplanting. It's almost painful, I know, to cut back those little green beauties. Still, you must. The roots of overcrowded seedlings will be impossible to untangle when you transplant. Also, nutrition will be inadequate and seedlings will become weak and spindly. Use small floral snips or manicure scissors to cut seedlings back, leaving a 2-inch space between seedlings. Pulling them can damage the roots of neighboring seedlings.

Graduation Time

When seedlings have two sets of true leaves, they're ready to be transplanted, either into the garden if the danger of frost has passed or into larger pots until it's safe to put them outside. A pot 2 inches in diameter is large enough for most seedlings. Lift a seedling out of the flat with a spoon or pie server, being careful to disturb the roots as little as possible. Hold the seedling by a cotyledon, *never* by its stem; if you damage the stem, you kill the plant. Don't worry if you damage a cotyledon; it falls off anyway. (If it already has, lift the seedling by a true leaf; the plant will grow more.)

Before planting seedlings outdoors, they need to be *hardened off*. This is gardening jargon for getting young plants acclimated to the cooler temps and higher light outdoors. Move the flats or pots outdoors to a protected spot, out of full sun and wind. Bring them in before you go to bed. Do this for a couple of days, watching the seedlings to make sure they don't get dried out by wind or burned by the sun. Next, move them into an unprotected position, with exposure equivalent to what they'll have in the ground. Again, bring them inside at night and repeat for a few days. Once seedlings have been hardened off — after about a week — they're ready to plant.

Plant seedlings at their original level; don't expose the roots or bury the stem. This is a good rule for transplanting in general. There are exceptions (see Expose the Crown, page 53), but you'll almost always want to maintain the original planting level for your plant. Seedlings will grow quickly, so give them enough room. Check the seed packet for suggestions on spacing. Water the new seedlings after planting and give their roots a few weeks to establish themselves before you start feeding.

Move seedlings into a larger pot after the true leaves appear.

By keeping plants that you're hardening off in a cart or wheelbarrow, you make it easy to move them in and out of the sun and wind.

Seeds That Are Easy to Start

Plant Name	Seed Size	Germination Time	Light/Dark	Where/When
Cilantro	Medium	7–10 days	Dark	Indoors in biodegradable pots
Cleome	Medium	7–14 days	Light	Indoors 4–6 weeks before last frost *or* outdoors after last frost
Foxglove	Very small	14–21 days	Light	Indoors 8–10 weeks before last frost *or* outdoors in June
Lamb's ear	Small	14–30 days	Light	Indoors 8–10 weeks before last frost
Larkspur	Medium	14–21 days	Dark	Direct sow outdoors October–April
Nicotiana	Very small	10–20 days	Light	Indoors 6–8 weeks before last frost *or* outdoors after last frost
Pansy	Small	14–21 days	Dark	Direct sow outdoors in July for fall *and* spring bloom
Sunflower	Large	10–14 days	Dark	Indoors 6–8 weeks before last frost *or* outdoors after last frost
Tomato	Medium	6–14 days	Dark	Indoors 8–10 weeks before last frost
Zinnia	Medium/Large (depending on type)	5–10 days	Dark	Indoors 6–8 weeks before last frost *or* outdoors after last frost

Start Seeds Indoors

You don't want to start the seeds too early, as seedlings grown too long indoors tend to be leggy and skinny. To decide when to start them, work backwards. Find out when your last frost date is. You can get this info from a local nursery or county extension office. If the last frost date is May 15, for example, and the seed packet says to start seeds 6 weeks before planting them outside, start the seeds at the beginning of March. (See also Last Frost Date, page 23.)

Pour seed-starting mix into a large container, add water, and stir. You may want to cover the mix and let it sit overnight so the water is fully absorbed. The mix should be moist enough to hold a clump when you squeeze it but not so wet that water drips out when you squeeze. Fill each flat (or pot) with soil and press it down firmly. The soil level should be ½ inch below the edge of the flat.

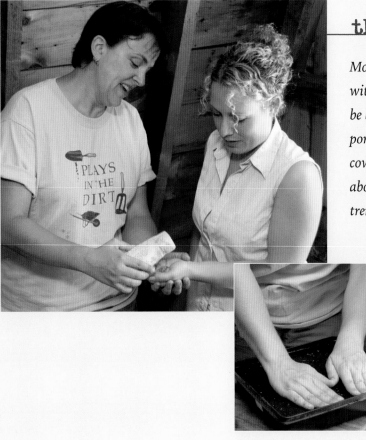

the cover-up

Most seeds don't require light to germinate, so cover them with potting mix. A good general rule is that seeds should be buried as deep as they are large. Very small seeds, like portulaca (Portulaca grandiflora), need only a very thin covering. If seeds are small, take a ruler and press a trench, about ¼ inch deep, into the mix. Scatter the seeds into the trench, then press the potting medium over them.

the big guys

Large seeds, like those of moonflower (Ipomoea alba), *which are the size of a kernel of corn, should be covered with about ¼ inch of potting mix. Poke holes in the mix with the end of a pencil or row marker. Make the holes about ½ inch deep and space them 2 inches apart. Place a seed in each hole and press the mix over the seed with your finger.*

light lovers

Some seeds, like those of snapdragon (Antirrhinum majus) and flowering tobacco (Nicotiana), require light to germinate. Use a plant marker to mark out a shallow trench, then sow the small seeds in the trench but leave them uncovered. Press larger seeds into the top of the mix, spaced appropriately.

settling in

Use row markers to label the seeds in each flat. Mist the soil surface with water to settle the seeds into place. Cover the flat or pot with a piece of plastic wrap or a piece of glass, or enclose the flat in a clear dry-cleaning bag. This keeps the humidity high. To water a seed flat (or pot), set the entire container in a pan of water about 2 inches deep. (The water shouldn't come over the top of the flat.) Let it sit for about a half hour to fully absorb moisture, then remove.

PLANTS

Invite Hummingbirds to Your Garden

3

Seeing red isn't always a bad thing. If you're a humming-bird, red is a welcome sight, an appetizing come-on to a nectar-licious meal. Although hummingbirds feed from flowers of all colors, they are inordinately tempted by the red and the tubular. I'm not sure why. Sure, I've read a few theories, but I don't have cold hard scientific facts to parade in front of you. All I can say is, these jewel-like fliers like tubular red flowers the most.

While sugar is an important hummingbird food, it is not the *most* important hummingbird food. Hummers require protein, which they get primarily from feeding

on small insects and occasionally pollen. But without nectar, hummers wouldn't have the energy to hunt for protein, so both are essential.

In addition to planting flowers to attract hummingbirds, you can also use hummingbird feeders. These range from inexpensive, plastic feeders to expensive, art glass models. Let your wallet be your guide. A sugar syrup (made of 1 part sugar to 4 parts water) is the appropriate food. Don't use honey. Honey ferments easily once it is diluted with water and a fungus dangerous to hummers can grow on fermented honey. Sugar syrup should be replaced every 3 to 5 days, depending on the temperature. If the syrup turns cloudy, it has spoiled; throw it out.

Hummingbirds have to eat all the time to stay alive; on average, every 10 minutes. They eat about two thirds of their body weight daily. Hummers are constantly exploring, always hunting for food. If you create an appealing hummingbird hot spot, they will find it.

In addition to plants and a feeder, set up a birdbath; hummers like to bathe in shallow water. Insects are also an important part of a balanced hummer diet, so insecticides are verboten in a hummingbird garden. An insect that has been poisoned becomes a poisonous meal for a hummingbird. Water, too, may become contaminated by insecticides. Just say no.

ETA

Male hummingbirds generally arrive first, staking out territory based on food availability. To find out when hummers will be in your area, check the hummingbird migration map online (see Resources in appendix). Females arrive a few weeks later than males and look for nesting spots. Both males and females are highly territorial, and it's not unusual for hummers to battle over nectar.

There's an old wives' tale that says by keeping your hummingbird feeder full, you may delay the departure of hummingbirds on their migration, causing them harm, perhaps even death. Not true. Hummingbirds will leave when it's time to leave; they are not easily swayed by the lure of a regular supply of sugar water. Still, leaving up a feeder may have other consequences. I once watched a bear rip my hummingbird feeder (and the branch it hung from) off the dogwood tree and drink from it as if it were a can of Red Bull, sugar syrup running down his furry black chest. If you're going to keep your feeder up when bears are awake and roaming (if you live in bear country, that is), make sure it's where they won't go. And when you figure out where that is, please e-mail me.

Classic Hummingbird Plants

Try a combination of annuals, perennials, and vines for a classic hummingbird garden. Hybrid flowers often produce less nectar than the species, so go for the old-fashioned types. And make sure to plant for a full season of bloom to keep hummingbirds in your garden as long as possible.

What follows is just a sampling to whet your appetite and the appetite of your local hummingbird population. Consider the salvias, red-hot poker, and Indian paintbrush. Think tubular, think reddish, and you're well on your way to creating a little piece of hummingbird heaven.

Beardtongues (*Penstemon* species and hybrids)

Beardtongues (*Penstemon* species and hybrids)

Beardtongues come in many colors, and all attract hummingbirds. They grow best in full sun and are drought tolerant. Height ranges from 1 to 3 feet tall. Planting beardtongue is an excellent way to add some different colors to your hummingbird garden. Zones 4 and 5.

Cardinal flower (*Lobelia cardinalis*)

A North American native, cardinal flower is perfect for a wet (perhaps even boggy), sunny to part-sunny spot. This stately perennial (to 4 feet tall) is a deeply saturated red; new hybrids come in every imaginable shade of pink and burgundy. Zone 3.

Cardinal flower (*Lobelia cardinalis*)

Cardinal vine *(Ipomoea quamoclit)*

Columbine *(Aquilegia canadensis)*

Fuchsias *(Fuchsia* hybrids and species)

Hyssops *(Agastache* hybrids)

Cardinal vine *(Ipomoea quamoclit)*

An annual vine for full sun, cardinal vine doesn't transplant well, so plant seed directly. In subsequent years the vine will self-seed. Small trumpet-shaped flowers are an intense deep red, and leaves are small, finely cut, and quite delicate. Annual.

Columbine *(Aquilegia canadensis)*

This native North American perennial grows best in part to full sun. Numerous delicate, red and yellow flowers perch above deeply lobed gray-green foliage. Hybrid columbines in many other colors are also attractive to hummers. Zone 4.

Fuchsias (*Fuchsia* hybrids and species)

Cool-weather annuals, fuchsias grow best in part shade with good air circulation. They come in many shades of orange, red, and pink. Upright forms grow well in containers and in the ground, and cascading forms are perfect in hanging baskets. Annual.

Hyssops (*Agastache* hybrids)

Hyssops come in many colors; they are all fragrant herbs with flowers that appeal to hummingbirds. In fact, hyssop is sometimes called hummingbird mint. These are xeric (xeriphytic or drought tolerant) plants that must have excellent drainage, and flowers will be most abundant in full sun. If you live in a rainy area but crave the fragrant hyssop, try more humidity-tolerant cultivars like 'Blue Fortune' and Korean hyssop. Zones 4–6.

Mexican catchfly *(Silene laciniata)*

A wildflower that demands to be left alone, Mexican catchfy should be planted in dry, infertile soil. Once established, it grows best when kept thirsty and hungry. (Remember, even xeric — aka drought-tolerant — plants need water to get established. (See How to Be Water-Wise, pages 67–71.) This is a full-sun plant with deep orange blossoms and fringed petals. It's as irresistible to humans as it is to hummers, although we tend not to sip from them. Zone 5.

Mexican catchfly *(Silene laciniata)*

Red bee balm *(Monarda didyma)*

This might as well be called red hummingbird balm. Yeah, not so catchy, but the birds seriously love this plant. Its flowers are composed of numerous red tubes and its foliage is quite fragrant. It spreads by underground runners and can be invasive, so keep an eye on it. Grow bee balm in full sun to part shade. Zone 4.

Red bee balm *(Monarda didyma)*

Red yucca *(Hesperaloe parviflora)*

A xeric classic, red yucca has stiff, swordlike leaves growing in a rosette. This succulent plant grows best in full sun. The plant itself is 2 to 3 feet tall, and the multi-flowered bloom spike tops out at 4 to 5 feet. Wet soil is a killer. Zone 5.

Red yucca *(Hesperaloe parviflora)*

Trumpet vine *(Campsis radicans)*

A fast-growing, drought-tolerant, full-sun plant, trumpet vine comes in red-flowered and yellow-flowered varieties, but the reds are more floriferous and more appealing to hummingbirds. An established plant will be blanketed with blooms and is a hummingbird magnet. Zone 4.

Trumpet vine *(Campsis radicans)*

Cold Frames: Extending the Growing Season

4

Once you've been bitten by the gardening bug, it's awfully difficult to recover, especially in early spring, when fresh green things are poking up everywhere and you yearn to get outside and start digging. It doesn't seem fair that you have to stay indoors, dreaming about what you're dying to plant.

The fact is that every gardener gets burned at least once. It hits 60°F in April and we're seduced by the tomato seedlings at the local nursery. We take them home and plant them. On May 1, the temperature drops into the 20s. What's a gardener to do?

When this happened to me, I ran a space heater out to the raised bed and covered the whole thing with tarps so my tomatoes wouldn't perish. That did the trick, but if I hadn't been home that night, I would have had to start my vegetables all over again.

Mother Nature gets the last word here. If it's too cold, it's too cold and there ain't nothin' you can do about it. Well, maybe there's one thing you can try to keep hoary Jack Frost from nipping at your buds. If you just can't wait till the date of the average last frost, build a cold frame to extend the growing season. A simple shelter, either assembled from found materials or built from a kit, will give you extra time on both sides of the growing season. In some zones, it may allow you to grow year-round.

Using Your Cold Frame

Temperature control is essential, and it doesn't take much for a cold frame to get too hot. Even in a Zone 6 winter, a closed cold frame can reach 90° to 100°F in full sun. A good rule of thumb is that if outdoor temps are in the 40s, prop open the lid 4 to 6 inches. If temps are in the 50s, take off the cover altogether. Before the sun sets, close or replace it in order to trap the heat inside the frame. On a really cold night, throw a blanket or a couple of beach towels over the transparent cover for extra insulation.

Last Frost Date

What *is* the average last frost date? For decades, government weather stations have collected data on climate and weather patterns. By analyzing this data, they've established average first and last frost dates to tell gardeners and farmers when it's safe to plant frost-tender plants. Check online or ask at a local nursery or your county extension office to find out what these dates are for your area. Summer annuals can be planted outdoors after the last frost date (but remember, this is an *average,* not a guarantee!) and you can expect the growing season to end for annuals on or about the first frost date in the fall. (See also page 12.)

Good Things Come in Small Boxes, Too

A cold frame box is more traditional, but there are several smaller, portable products to consider, especially for temporary protection. Individual, transparent bell jars and plastic tents accomplish the same things as a cold frame — that is, they protect plants from cold temperatures and wind, they allow for ventilation, and they accumulate warmth.

The bottom half of a plastic gallon jug or a small solar bell acts like an old-fashioned bell jar by creating a zone of warmth around each plant. Cover a group of seedlings or a single larger plant with a plastic umbrella cloche.

Of course I *do* have a hammer, but I never took shop in junior high, so I'm not entirely sure what to do with it. If you have mad carpentry skills, consider building a more permanent cold frame from rot-resistant wood such as cedar or cypress. By cutting the top edges of the side pieces at an angle, you provide the slope needed for sun to penetrate the transparent cover. Mound some soil around the base of the frame to prevent bottom drafts.

If you really want to get fancy, consider an automatic vent opener. As temperatures rise and fall throughout the day, the hinged cover of the frame will open and close . . . like magic! These vent openers work with a beeswax cartridge that expands when heated by the sun, opening the vent. No electricity is required.

A portable cold-frame kit is lightweight and oh-so-easy to assemble.

A cold frame is perfect for hardening off seedlings (see Graduation Time, page 12); just place the flats or pots inside the frame. You can also grow cool-weather crops like lettuces directly in the soil inside the frame. For an early-spring treat, plant a pot of spring bulbs and keep the pot in the frame for 6 weeks of chilling before you bring it indoors to sprout. (See Forcing Spring Bulbs, page 2.)

If you buy a portable kit, you can make it into a mobile hot zone. Simply place the frame over a section of garden that needs extra warmth and remove it when the seedlings under it have toughened up.

Choose the Perfect Garden Spot

What's the first thing to do in your garden before planting anything? If you said, "Dig a hole," I'm sorry, but you're wrong! First, take a long walk around your yard (or a short walk around your deck) and ask yourself a few questions. This section is all about location, location, location.

There are several things to consider when choosing your perfect garden spot. You'll need to think about light and shade, high and low temperatures, humidity, rainfall, and exposure to winds. Does this sound overwhelming? Let's break it down into manageable chunks.

Let the Sun Shine In . . . or Not

What does "sunny" mean to a plant? Yes, this is a little tricky, but it's not rocket science. You'll need to make a few observations over several days' time to assess how much sunlight your plant(s) will get. If the spot gets 6 to 8 hours of direct sun during the day, you may officially deem this *full sun*. If it gets 4 hours of direct sun and indirect light for the rest of the day, this is a *part-sun* position. If it gets no direct sun and only indirect light, this is *part shade*. A spot in the woods, shaded by a canopy of high trees is just plain *shady*.

Those are the easy ones, the cut-and-dried, the black and white. Of course, it's the shades of gray (literally) that complicate matters. Relax. Make your most educated guess. If you make a mistake, you can dig up the plant and put it somewhere else. Really.

Baby, It's Cold Outside

What's your hardiness zone? The United States Department of Agriculture (USDA) has divided the United States into zones based on average minimum winter temperatures. Plants are rated as hardy to a particular zone,

Microclimate Matters

Any given location may also be affected by microclimates, which can affect your zone. For instance:

Elevation. The map shows my house in Pennsylvania as being in Zone 6. But at 1,200' I'm high enough and exposed to enough wind that I plant for Zone 5 to be safe.

Exposure to winds. Neighboring buildings and trees can make a difference. Winds speed the evaporation of moisture from leaves; a yard surrounded by trees or buildings will be protected from drying winds.

Protective walls. A southern wall retains solar energy, and is often the warmest spot in the garden. If you covet a plant that needs extra protection, try it here.

Valleys. Cold air settles in valleys, so if your yard contains a hill, the temps will be cooler at the bottom.

Shade. In summer, a shaded area of your garden can be up to 20 degrees cooler than a nearby sunny spot.

You don't have to memorize all these details immediately, but keep them in the back of your mind. To start out, learn your hardiness zone and check the zone rating for any plant you want to buy.

which means they can survive the minimum temperature in that zone. For example, a plant hardy to Zone 5 can withstand winter temperatures of -20°F. Additionally, some plants actually require a certain amount of cold to grow well. Locate your zone on a map, online (see appendix, page 238), or by asking at a local nursery.

When you're plant shopping, check the plant's tag to confirm that your intended purchase is suited to your zone. Don't assume just because a nearby nursery is selling something that it's hardy for you.

If you're buying annuals you won't see a hardiness zone on the tag. The reason for this is that annuals live only for a year, no matter where they grow. They complete their life cycles in a single year, so the issue of winter survival isn't important. But perennials, trees, and shrubs should all have their hardiness zones listed on the tags.

Where Things Heat Up

If you live in a warm climate, you should also understand the Heat Zone Map of the American Horticultural Society (AHS). Just as some plants are more cold tolerant than others, so are some more resistant to heat stress. The AHS has divided the country into zones according to how many days the temperature exceeds 86°F. This is the temperature above which most plants exhibit heat stress. AHS heat zones are most relevant for the southern states; if you live in the northern part of the United States, you can pretty much ignore them.

Into Each Life a Little Rain . . .

It's also important to have a general idea about your rainfall and humidity. If you live in the arid Southwest, you'll want drought-tolerant plants. If you live in the cool and humid Northwest, not so much. Maybe you need plants that can take consistently moist soils, or plants that tolerate drying winds. These are all characteristics of climate that affect your gardening choices. If this seems like a lot to consider, don't worry, it'll soon be second nature. Picking the right plants for your location is the first step toward success in the garden.

NYC is generally considered Zone 6, but on this 17th floor terrace, I plant for Zone 5. Higher elevation = more wind and colder air. Classic microclimate!

Hanging Baskets: Costume Jewelry of the Garden World

6

Hanging baskets are the costume jewelry of the garden world, and you can quote me on that. Here's why: When your garden is planted, the flowers are blooming, and the mulch has been laid, you still need something more. Your garden isn't quite finished. It's like when you get dressed for a special event: the shoes, the clothes, the hair are all perfect. But you still need just the right earring(s).

I can't explain why we humans feel the need to take plants out of the ground where they grow all by themselves and move them into unlikely spots like hanging

Even though I adore hanging baskets, I'm not going to lie to you: this kind of horticultural hubris comes with a price. A hanging basket requires extra care for several reasons. First of all, it's exposed to the sun, wind, and cold on all sides, so it dries out quickly. Second, part of the appeal of a hanging basket is the abundant, overflow effect. A fully planted basket has reduced room for soil, retains less water, and needs more frequent water and fertilizer. Ah, but the rewards are so rewarding.

baskets. (I *can* tell you we've been doing it for centuries. Ever hear of the Hanging Gardens of Babylon?) Maybe because it's just plain fun.

A hanging basket is the perfect garden ornament for a quick makeover. Are you feeling cool? Choose lobelia, scaevolla, browallia, and helichrysum. Maybe you're hot! hot! hot! Combine orange calibrachoa, yellow lantana, and fuchsia 'Gartenmeister'. Or change plantings with the season: pansies and violets in spring, snapdragons and diascia in fall. The point is to garden in the moment, to plant what you feel, man.

Lots of nurseries sell pre-planted hanging baskets, but if you want an extra-special combination, something that reflects your personal genius, plant your own. It's a challenge, but limited space encourages innovation as you combine colors and shapes in a compact area. Anyone can choose great plants for a 20-foot perennial border. Finding the perfect combination of three or four plants for a 12-inch hanging basket, however . . . now *that's* an accomplishment!

Not All Baskets Are Equal

There are innumerable kinds of containers suitable for hanging, from plastic baskets to old birdcages. I scour flea markets for old-fashioned milk-bottle carriers, egg baskets, galvanized pails. If you can hang it and punch holes in it, you can plant in it.

The traditional plastic pot requires the least maintenance because it's nonporous and thus retains moisture longer. If you use a basketlike item instead, you'll need to line it to keep soil from washing away. Buy a coir (coconut fiber) liner, or make your own from pieces of sheet moss. A plastic liner inside the coir or moss helps keep potting mix moist; just be sure to poke drainage holes in it every few inches.

What's a Good Mix?

A lightweight potting mix is crucial. Yes, it will dry out more quickly than a heavier mix does, but it's your best bet for keeping the weight of your container manageable. Believe me now or believe me when you're lifting those

fully planted and freshly watered containers back onto their brackets above your head.

Depending on your plant and container choice, consider adding hydrogels to reduce watering. Hydrogels increase the amount of water a potting mix can retain, so you water less often. They hold hundreds of times their weight in water (literally) and gradually release it to the plants' roots. Remember, hydrate the granules first, add them to the potting mix, *then* plant. (See Hydrogels, page 70, to discover how I messed this up and looked like an idiot.)

A Feeding Plan

A good general rule is to fertilize once every 2 weeks. Choose a fertilizer with its middle number higher than the other two numbers (for example, 15-30-15). This indicates a bloom-booster, and we're trying to pump up the flowering jam here.

At the nursery, check plant labels and choose plants that will be happy in the light conditions you can give them.

A coir (coconut fiber) liner keeps soil from falling between the slats of this half basket. The natural fiber also adds nice texture and color to your display.

When It Comes to the Plants

When selecting plants, look for varying growth habits. The general rule for planting a successful container is to include a thriller, a spiller, and a filler. The thriller is usually an upright with unusual foliage, like a spiky angelonia or a tall caladium. The spiller might be a silver helichrysum or cascading calibrachoa. The filler can be any number of things to beef up your planting: cool, blue lobelia; multicolored coleus; or a beauteous begonia. If your basket will be viewed from all angles, place the tallest plants at the center. If the basket will be seen from one side only, use the tall plants at the back. Leave an inch between the top of the soil and the rim of the container, so you won't spill when watering. Water thoroughly, and if your basket has a saucer attached to it, tip out any water that accumulates there before you hang the basket in place.

Keep It Clean!

Meticulous maintenance (feeding, watering, pruning, and deadheading) is key; a shaggy basket is a shameful thing. Another way to keep things fresh is to replace annuals as they pass their prime. If you started the season with pansies surrounded by ivy, replace the pansies with verbena in June, then dahlias in September.

Be attentive to your hanging baskets. They may not last as long as a favorite piece of jewelry, but a few creative containers can perfectly accessorize your outdoor living space. And you wouldn't want to be seen in public without your flowers on.

Intensive Care

The soil in hanging baskets dries out more quickly than soil in other containers. If (by some fluke) you forget to water and the soil in a basket dries out so much that it pulls away from the edges, soak the entire basket in a tub of water for 30 minutes to hydrate the potting mix. If you can't soak the basket, water it thoroughly every 2 hours until the soil has expanded fully.

Pot Up a Hanging Basket

lay 'em out

Gather all your plants and supplies together. A traditional plastic basket requires the least maintenance because it's nonporous, and retains moisture longer. A plastic pot is also a light-weight choice.

lush is more

Place one plant right next to the other for a chock-full, spilling-over-the-edge effect.

dying of thirst

Remember: Hanging plants are exposed to the sun, wind, and cold on all sides so they dry out quickly. Water them well when you plant them, and keep them well watered throughout the season.

7

Raised-Bed

Gardens

Raised beds rule — no two ways about it! I'd think so even if I didn't garden in Rock City, Pennsylvania. I admit my town isn't really called Rock City. That's just my term of endearment for a place where the soil is rockier than I could have imagined possible. The benefits of a raised bed go far beyond saving labor. (Although any time I can leave the pickax in the shed, I'm a happy gardener.) A raised bed offers you rock-free gardening and so much more. Among the many perks raised beds offer, these are the tops:

✿ **Warmth.** Soil in a raised bed gets warm earlier and stays warm later than the soil in your garden. This gives you a longer growing season.

✿ **Drainage** is superior in a raised bed (unless you pack it full of clay). In fact, a low spot where water collects can be made productive by raising the soil level.

✿ **Ideal soil.** You mix the soil for a raised bed, ensuring adequate nutrition and workable texture.

✿ **Access.** For people with limited mobility, raised beds are easier to work than in-ground beds (not so much squatting and bending).

✿ **No compaction.** The soil in a raised bed gets very little foot traffic and therefore very little compaction. Not only does this make it easier to work the soil, but weeding is also less difficult.

✿ **Soil depth.** Some urban gardens have a *very* thin layer of topsoil. (I've dug into backyards where there's concrete just 4 inches below the lawn.) A raised bed gives you the added soil depth you need without renting a jackhammer (and the requisite jackhammer operator).

These raised beds in Boston's Fenway community gardens make it easier for gardeners with limited mobility to enjoy their plants.

A Leg Up on Pest Control

If burrowing animals are wreaking havoc with your garden, line the bottom and sides of the raised bed with galvanized chicken wire and put in a layer of gravel. This will slow chipmunks, voles, and other animals that might dig up into your garden from below ground.

If birds are the bane of your existence, hang netting over your raised bed when your crop begins to ripen. Place a post or stake at each corner of your bed, and drape netting over the stakes to protect berries and other fruit from flying thieves.

This commercially made raised bed is easy to assemble.

(Almost) Instant Beds

The easiest way to make a raised bed is simply to pile up dirt. If you're going to raise the height of the soil by just a few inches (4 to 6, max) you don't need to construct walls. To create a raised bed where there's now lawn, spread a layer of newspaper to help smother grass and weeds, then pile soil on top of the newspaper. Firm it into a mound, then plant. This will be perfect for annuals and herbs. You'll probably have to reshape the edges from year to year as traffic and weather have their way with the soil, but this is the down and dirtiest way to grow in a raised bed.

Wall It Off

For greater planting depth, you'll need some kind of wall. The height of the bed will depend on what you want to grow; most garden vegetables and lots of flowering perennials are perfectly happy with 8 to 10 inches of soil. If you're going to plant carrots, potatoes, or another root crop, give yourself at least 12 inches of soil depth. (A bed deeper than 12 inches will need a foundation and support structure. We're not getting into anything that complicated here.)

By keeping the beds relatively narrow (no wider than 4 feet), you'll be able to reach into the center of a bed from either side. A raised bed that will be accessible from only one side should be about 2 feet wide. Rectangular beds are practical, efficient, and well suited to growing vegetables and cut flowers. You can plant tightly (leaving no space for paths) and use every inch of soil for maximum production. If you're thinking of making all your garden beds raised beds, feel free to incorporate some curves.

Raised beds can be as fancy or as simple as you like. If you're a carpenter and gravitate toward working with wood, use something rot resistant (like redwood, cedar, or cypress) so you don't have to replace the boards often. Some old, dried-out railroad ties are safe, but newer ties may ooze creosote, so don't use them.

Any raised bed with a wooden frame needs reinforced corners, either internal or external. Simply nailing the boards together isn't adequate;

Rebar stakes (above) are pounded into the ground to hold the boards for the raised bed (above left) in place.

they'll pull apart within a year. Use galvanized metal braces and screws, or small wooden posts screwed inside the corners of the frame. There are also adjustable-corner kits that attach to stakes that you pound into the ground. Slide the boards into the corner pieces to complete the frame.

If carpentry isn't your bag, try cinder block or stone (brick also works for a short bed). By keeping the wall height under 12 inches, you won't need mortar or cement. Plant the center holes in the cinder blocks with small herbs or flowers; it looks totally cool.

Starting Small

If you want to start small, use an old tire to create a mini raised bed. A single tire is deep enough to grow most annuals, and two tires, stacked, provide enough root space for a large tomato. It's a great way to grow heat-loving crops like tomatoes, peppers, and eggplant. Remember, black rubber absorbs *a lot* of heat, so anything planted in a tire will need frequent watering, perhaps daily.

If you're not comfortable with the idea of having old tires piled up around your front yard or deck, a whiskey barrel is just as good. You'll get enough planting space to grow a combination of annual foliage and flowers, or, for the more practical, a collection of herbs, two peppers, or a single tomato. (A whiskey barrel is even deep enough to accommodate an experimental tuber or two.) For drainage, drill three 1-inch holes in the bottom of the barrel before planting.

All kinds of raised-bed kits are available, from faux fieldstone to precut cedar with decorative corner pieces. Make your selection based on the style of your home and how much you want to spend. Whichever way you go, the improved drainage of a raised bed means the soil dries out more quickly, so be sure to mulch and stay on top of the watering.

Making Your Bed

Site preparation is simple. Be aware of the surrounding landscape. Don't put a raised bed where the added soil depth may suffocate tree roots.

Make sure the ground is level. If you're building on grass, either remove the sod, or cover it with newspaper before adding soil. (This will cut down on weeds, and allow the roots from the plants to run deep.) Next, lay out the block or stone, or assemble and place the wooden frame. Fill the bed with a mixture of compost and topsoil and you're ready to plant.

A whisky barrel makes an ideal small planting bed.

Cool Tools 8

I love my tools like most women love their shoes. You don't necessarily have to share my passion for useful implements, but the right tool can make a tough job an awful lot easier.

So what do you need? That depends on the texture of your soil. If you're working in very rocky earth, you'll need a mattock or grub ax. Anywhere, you'll need a good shovel, a pair of pruners, a trowel, and gloves.

My soil is bad. Not malevolent or naughty, but nutrient poor and difficult to work with. I've amended it with potash, manure, leaf mold, and greensand, and the soil

Where I live, a girl's best friend is a mattock — great for loosening earth and prying up stones.

So many spades ... so little time.

has improved over the years. But I can't plant anything without using a mattock; in my garden, there's as much rock as there is soil.

A Girl's Best Friend: A Mattock

I wouldn't be surprised if you don't know what a mattock is. I certainly didn't before I moved to Rock City, PA. Agriculture isn't big in this part of the state. But adversity breeds ingenuity, and dealing with this stony soil has inspired me to get creative. I use containers and raised beds when I can't get past the rocks, and I always keep my mattock handy.

Some people call it a grub ax, but the visual image produced by the word "grub" is one I try to avoid. A mattock is like a pickax, but with a blade on each end. One blade is rotated 90 degrees, so it's perpendicular to the other. The horizontal blade is used to break up hard earth and pry up large stones. The vertical blade is used to chop roots and clods of dirt. You swing this tool like ol' John Henry; there's nothing dainty about it. (Do remember, however, that John Henry's heart exploded when he was racing that steam drill. I suggest you don't push yourself quite that hard.) I bought my mattock at a flea market and it's quite heavy. The extra weight and leverage of a long wooden handle helps you get a good swing. There are shorter versions for less-heavy work. Or if you're weak.

Shovels and Spades

Obviously you can't plant without a shovel, but what kind of shovel you choose is perhaps not so obvious. One of my first teachers (Mike Ruggiero, this means you) told me to buy the most expensive tools I could afford. I scoffed, but now must admit he was right. A quality tool feels good in your hands and gives you years of loyal service; a cheap tool breaks and needs to be replaced, ultimately costing more. The key is to buy what you can afford. Don't ratchet up the credit-card debt to buy the Rolls Royce of shovels if you're on a Kia budget.

My favorite shovel is actually a spade. It has a 36-inch wooden handle with a D grip and a long (18"), narrow (5"), slightly curved blade. It's called a transplant shovel or a trenching shovel because it goes deep. (It's the one on the far left in the photo on page 43.) When you're transplanting something in the garden, a trenching shovel minimizes root disturbance. A fiberglass handle is lighter than a wooden handle, so if weight is an issue, consider this. Wood, on the other hand, is less expensive and appeals to my aesthetic sense. Either must be strong enough to handle some real weight. You're going to be leaning on it with all you've got.

Some people find a long-handled shovel more to their liking than a spade. The blade is rounded and wide and moves more earth per shovelful than a transplant spade. Your choice will depend on the kind of work you're doing, and you may eventually want both. Try out a few styles before making a commitment.

A Cut Above: Your Pruners

There are two basic kinds of pruners: bypass and anvil. Bypass are better. One blade *passes by* the second to make a clean cut, like scissors. Stem tissue is severed neatly with as little trauma as possible (considering you're amputating a limb). Anvil pruners cut by coming together: one narrow-edged blade presses hard against a second blade with a flat surface. This compresses the stem tissue. If you're cutting up dead wood, this is fine. If you're pruning a live plant, and want subsequent growth to continue from your pruning point, you need the branches and stems to be healthy, not mangled. And if you're cutting flowers for an arrangement, you want the stem tissue intact so water can travel up it. Go for the bypass pruners.

Handle design is important to personal comfort. Some rotate, some are stationary. Sizes vary. Check out different grips and weights to find the best pruner for your hand.

Trowel Power

A sharp trowel is invaluable. You may need a shovel or spade to plant most perennials, but a trowel is my tool of choice for planting annuals and working in containers. It's quick, it's down, it's dirty, and perfect for multiple,

Bypass pruners make a clean cut that's better for the health of your plants.

This inexpensive glove clip has saved many pairs of gloves from being inadvertently left behind!

quick, small holes. I prefer a molded rubber handle; it's easy on the hands. Some people like wooden handles but they tend to give me blisters after about an hour. And forget about those trowels with metal handles . . . pretty, not practical.

Hand in Glove

There are lots of different kinds of gloves to choose from; make your choice based on comfort and protection. Some people like the breathability of cloth with rubber grips for a firm hold. Others prefer soft and supple kidskin. Me, I like a washable leather glove for maximum protection and easy clean-up. I also have this really cool glove accessory. It clips onto my belt loop and holds the gloves so I won't lose them. (I tend to walk away from any tool not attached to my body.) Of all the tools I own (and you can imagine how many that is), the glove clip is the one that gets the most covetous comments.

These tools will get you started and well on your way. And if you find yourself getting especially attached to a spade or a mattock, don't say I didn't warn you!

A Cautionary Tale

For years I resisted wearing gloves. I didn't mind getting dirty and I needed to *feel* the soil and roots in order to enjoy my work. Then one day I was digging up a shrub for my mother. It was a tenacious quince, reluctant to give up its hold on its small patch of earth. After removing the plant intact (it lives on in my own garden), I set about working on the remaining roots. I dug and I leaned and I pried. I fell, not at all gracefully. I looked at my hand. My middle finger was pierced by a quince twig the size of a pencil. In one side and out the other. It throbbed, it swelled, it hurt. If my sister and her husband (both doctors) hadn't been visiting, I would have had to go to the ER. As it was, they took me to their office, gave me anesthesia, sliced open my finger, and removed the stick. This all could have been avoided (except for the indignity of my fall) if I'd worn gloves. Which I now do with the zeal of a convert.

Cool Tools

From left to right: Transplant shovel, garden shovel, two axes, pry bar, small and large mattocks.

Plant a Container Tree

9

What's that? You don't actually *have* a garden? Well, that doesn't condemn you to a life of treelessness. Many trees do well in containers, and growing a containerized tree gives you lots of options. Start with the best possible soil (see It Ain't Just Dirt, page 216) and place your container in the best possible location. If you've misjudged your light, you can move the container, rather than dig up the tree. There are a few special requirements for growing in containers, of course, but the process is *much* easier than most people think.

Some Quirks of Container-Grown Trees

When you choose your tree, remember that trees grown in containers will be considerably smaller than their in-ground counterparts. For example, a Juneberry may reach 40' in nature but top out at 20' in a large container (40" l × 24" w × 36" h). Limiting root size limits top growth.

A tree in a container is more vulnerable to cold temperatures than its in-ground counterpart, because its roots are insulated by a much smaller volume of soil. Give the root-ball 6 to 8 inches of soil on all sides as insulation from the cold. Add that to the dimensions of the root-ball to determine what size container you need.

Rooftop container gardeners need to be especially aware of windy conditions. The higher up you go, the windier it gets on most city terraces and the more dried out plant tissue will get. Plus, the only thing separating the

Underplant a container tree with ground cover for a lush look.

Excellent Trees to Grow in Pots

Botanical Name	Common Name	Mature Height	Winning Characteristics	Hardiness Zones
Acer japonicum, A. palmatum	Japanese maple, full moon maple	20'–30'	Wide range of interesting shapes (weeping and upright) and leaf colors	5–8 (depending on variety)
Amelanchier arborea, A. × grandiflora	Juneberry, Serviceberry, Shadblow	20'–40'	White flowers, delicious berries	4–9
Cercis canadensis	Redbud	20'–30'	Bright pink buds cover the branches before leaves emerge; good in shade	4–9
Chamaecyparis obtusa	False cypress	50'–75'	Soft-needled evergreen; great texture and shape	4–8
Cornus kousa	Kousa dogwood	20'–30'	Large flowers in spring; large, tasty berries in fall	5–8
Cupressus arizonica 'Blue Ice'	Cypress	10'–12'	Intense blue-gray, spidery flat needles; cool cones	6–9
Lagerstroemia indica	Crape myrtle	15'–25'	Unending summer bloom; alluring bark	6–9
Malus hybrids	Crab apples	15'–25'	Spring flowers, fall berries	4–8 (depending on variety)
Pinus parviflora 'Glauca'	Japanese white pine	25'–50'	Blue-green needles; interesting tree form; cool cones	4–7
Prunus cerasifera	Purple-leaf plum	10'–20'	Deep purple foliage	5–8
Syringa meyeri	Meyer lilac	6'–12'	Mildew-free foliage; profuse bloom	3–7

Loving Care

You have lots of choices about what trees to plant in containers and where to put them, but you really don't have much choice about how you water. If your tree is in a container, you *must* have irrigation. Container plants dry out more quickly than plants in the ground. They have a much smaller volume of soil from which to extract moisture. Water evaporates through the sides of the container as well as from the soil surface and the leaves; in the heat of summer, container plants may need watering every day. Hence, I repeat: If containers, then irrigation. (See pages 121–124 for advice on irrigation systems.)

tree's roots from the frigid air is a small volume of soil and the container's thin walls. To be safe, subtract a zone or two from whatever the map shows as your hardiness zones, if you're above the third floor. If you live in Zone 7, and your terrace is on the 10th floor, plant for Zone 5 or 6.

If your container will be on a deck or terrace, make sure the floor is strong enough to support the combined weight of the container, the tree, and wet soil. If your container will stand on cement, brick, or asphalt you can pretty much just go ahead and choose a spot that suits you and your traffic pattern.

This sleek container perfectly complements the strong lines of the pine tree.

Pot Up a Tree

You need a few tools and supplies for planting your container: drainage material (see page 48), landscape cloth or screening, and maybe a staple gun. Oh, and a container.

If you live in an area where winter temps go below freezing, make sure your container is frost resistant. Most terra-cotta is **not,** although several coats of a water sealant can increase its lifespan. Porous containers absorb water, and repeated freezing and thawing throughout the winter may cause them to crack. Some very expensive (but also very beautiful) terra-cotta is frost-proof. Ask before you buy. Wood and fiberglass are durable and there are some interesting, attractive new polymer/plastic pots that overwinter well.

You shouldn't have to worry about the pH or soil texture of your planting mix, as long as you buy a reputable brand. Most mixes are combinations of soil and lightweight organic matter. If you're planting on a terrace or rooftop where weight is restricted, be sure to choose a lightweight mix. Check the list of ingredients for any commercial soil you use. Some include fertilizer, and if this is the case, you won't need additional plant food for about a year.

hole in one

The first thing to do is to check to see if your container has holes in the bottom for drainage. A container without drainage holes is like a cat carrying case without air holes . . . so don't plant a tree in a container you can't drill holes in! It's easy to drill through wood, terra-cotta, fiberglass, or plastic. Use a sharp, 1-inch drill bit, and always be careful with power tools.

cover up

Cut a piece of landscape cloth to cover the holes. If you're using a wooden container, staple the cloth to the sides or bottom; if the container is made of plastic or fiberglass, just lay the cloth along the bottom.

the layered look

Add a layer of drainage material on top of the cloth. If you're gardening on a terrace or balcony where weight is a concern, use something lightweight like Styrofoam peanuts (not water-soluble cornstarch peanuts!). If your container sits on the ground you can use something heavier, like gravel. This layer facilitates drainage of excess water away from the root-ball, so roots won't stay soggy and rot. The depth of the drainage layer varies by the size of the container. If you're planting a good-sized tree in a 36-inch container, you'll want at least 6 inches of drainage material. A small shrub in an 18-inch container will be fine with 2 to 3 inches.

double duty

On top of the drainage layer, place another piece of landscape cloth. Again, if you're planting in wood, staple the cloth to the sides of the container. The soil will go on top of this second layer of cloth, which serves a dual purpose: It keeps the soil from washing away through the drainage material with repeated waterings, and if you're using Styrofoam peanuts, it keeps the peanuts from floating up through the soil over time.

setting the tree

Fill the container with enough soil to raise the tree to the appropriate level. When planting (a tree, a perennial, an annual), always maintain the original soil level of the plant. Planting too high exposes roots and planting too deep can deprive them of oxygen. Position the tree and fill in around the root-ball with soil, watering as you go and firming in the tree.

watering in

Water until water runs out of the bottom of the container.

DOWN &
DIRTY
PLANTS

Grow
Strawberries
...and Eat Them!

10

"Would mam'selle care for dessert? Some fresh strawberry sorbet, perhaps? Eet ees smooth, sensual, sophisticated, just like you, mam'selle."

Yes, impress your friends and neighbors by serving them strawberry sorbet. And impress them even more when you tell them you grew the berries yourself. It's remarkably simple to crank out (literally) a rich (and can it be fat-free?!) dessert, and also to grow the sweet little berries that make it all possible.

The first time I planted strawberries was as a ground cover on a terrace overlooking Central Park. I like to

Your Cooperative Extension office is *not* a socialist gardeners' collective. It's an extension of a local (usually state) land grant university, and the reason for its existence is to assist local gardeners and gardens. Co-op extension offices run many programs, among them the Master Gardener Program which educates gardeners, then enlists them as volunteers in the community. Almost every county has an Extension office that provides a gardeners' hotline once a week. Call them with your questions; it's what they're there for.

work early in the day, and thought a simple breakfast of fresh, sweet berries would be an excellent reward for a hardworking gardener (me). Of course, you can't grow a lot of strawberries in 3 square feet, but it's still a crop that delights.

Not All Strawberries Are Alike

Wherever you grow strawberries, there are a few things to consider. First, what kind of berries do you want to grow?

❀ **June-bearing berries** (aka spring-bearing berries) produce a single crop each year, during 3 to 6 weeks in spring. They put out numerous runners, which are worked back into the strawberry patch to keep it vigorous. If you have a good-sized garden plot and you want to make jam, wine, or anything else requiring a lot of fruit, plant June-bearing strawberries for a big crop all at once.

❀ **Day-neutral and everbearing strawberries** both produce smaller fruit than the June-bearing strawberries. Day-neutral strawberries produce fruit throughout the growing season and generate a few runners. They do especially well in the northern half of the United States. Everbearing strawberries produce two or three crops per year and not many runners.

They produce fewer berries than day-neutrals but tolerate warm climates better. Both can be grown in much smaller spaces, containers, a raised bed, or as a ground cover or edging plant.

Different strawberries are hardy to different zones, and your local Cooperative Extension office will be able to recommend the best species of each type of strawberry for your growing area. Seriously, the people who work there live for this kind of question. Volunteer Master Gardeners are standing by to field your call. I kid you not.

Berry Savvy

Strawberries are full-sun plants: they need at least 6 hours of sun per day. The more sun they get, the more flowers and fruit the plants produce. They are shallow rooted and need between 1 and 2 inches of water per week during active growth (an excellent crop for drip irrigation; see page 124).

Strawberries grow best in a slightly acid soil. Don't plant them near tomatoes, peppers, or potatoes, because those plants may carry verticillium rot (a soilborne fungal disease), which can decimate a strawberry patch. Plant strawberries as soon as you can work the soil in spring, usually in March or April.

Growing June-Bearing Strawberries

June-bearing plants require a little more labor than do everbearing or day-neutral, but I think they're worth it for the overflow of bounty. (I'm big on quantity.) Plant June-bearers in distinct rows 4 feet apart, with plants spaced 12 inches apart. As runners are produced, weave them back into the main patch, forming a matted row of plants about 18 inches wide. In the first year, pinch off all the flowers. I know this is heartbreakingly difficult, but if you're strong, you'll have more berries the following year.

After the bountiful second-year harvest, it's time for renovation. Pull out the lawn mower and mow the patch to a height of 1 to 1½ inches above the crowns. Shape the rows to be about 12 inches wide, digging up and tilling under any plants that have spread beyond their rows. Thin the plants to one every 6 inches and fertilize with a balanced plant food (see It Ain't Just Dirt, page 216). Continue to water throughout the season. This kind of care and attention will keep a patch productive for 3 or 4 years, if you continue to add organic amendments to the soil. When production falls off, it's time to replant the patch entirely.

Growing Everbearing and Day-Neutral Strawberries

Everbearing and day-neutral strawberries can be planted in clumps or rows, with plants spaced 8 to 10 inches apart. Remove any runners to keep the

Expose the Crown

Strawberries aren't usually grown from seed; you'll probably purchase a bunch of bare-root plants or perhaps some small potted runners. All strawberries should be planted with the crowns just above soil level. The crown (about an inch long) is the part of the plant between the roots and the stems. It's a series of buds from which leaves and stems emerge. Place the plants so their roots are covered, but the crown and leaves are above soil level, even though this may look a little high to you.

When strawberries are at their height, you can enjoy them by the bucketful. But don't wait too long before eating or preserving them.

main plants large and vigorous. Pinch off flowers that appear during the first 6 weeks (focusing plant energy on root and shoot growth), then let them bloom freely. You'll get a crop the first year. Day-neutrals produce well for about 2 years; everbearing, for 3.

Some gardeners suggest treating day-neutral plants as annuals, planting them anew every year. This is convenient where winters are too cold for strawberries, and also in some very mild climates. Where winter temps stay above 50°F, you can plant strawberries in fall, then harvest like crazy throughout the next growing season. No renovation is required for these strawberries.

All strawberries need a good winter mulch. Make sure to cover the crowns with at least 6 inches of straw or leaves. June-bearing varieties produce their buds in fall, so a late-spring frost could damage your crop. Don't let this happen!

Strawberry Pot

Strawberry pots are multi-level containers with pockets of various heights built into their sides. You can plant the top with spring-bearing plants, then pin runners to the soil in the lower side pockets, or you can plant each side pocket and the top opening with non-runner producing plants. Either way, you get a pot full of berries; not enough for a batch of jam, but still a joy to pick and eat in the warm, spring sun.

I Scream, You Scream, We All Scream for Ice Cream

Once picked, strawberries are delicate creatures; they'll keep in the refrigerator for just 2 or 3 days. Don't wash the berries until you're ready to use them. If you're not going to eat them before they get mushy, flash-freeze them. Gently rinse the berries, let them dry, and place them on a baking sheet, making sure no two berries touch. Put the entire sheet in the freezer. When the berries are frozen solid, transfer them to a container or ziplock bag.

Okay, you've planted, tended, and harvested. Now it's time for . . . ice cream! Or perhaps a refreshing sorbet for mam'selle?

Strawberry Sorbet

Makes 1 pint

½ cup water	2 tablespoons fresh lemon juice
½ cup sugar	2 tablespoons corn syrup
2 cups strawberries	

1. Make a simple syrup by combining the water and sugar, bringing it to a boil, then simmering until the sugar dissolves. Remove from the heat and refrigerate to cool.
2. Mash the strawberries and lemon juice into a pulp. If seeds bug you, push the mash through a strainer.
3. Combine the strawberries with the cooled simple syrup and the corn syrup. Pour the mixture into an ice-cream maker and proceed according to the manufacturer's instructions.

Strawberry Ice Cream

Makes 1 pint

1 egg	¼ teaspoon pure vanilla extract
⅓ cup sugar	1 cup heavy cream
1 cup fresh strawberries	

1. Beat together the sugar and egg until the mixture is thick and cream-colored.
2. Mash the strawberries and add them to the sugar mixture. Stir in the cream and vanilla.
3. Pour the mix into an ice-cream maker and proceed according to the manufacturer's instructions.

11

Grow-Bags: Easy, Instant Gardens

The first apartment my husband, Michael, and I shared was a single-room, fifth-floor walk-up on the Upper West Side. It wasn't as if we had much choice, New York City real estate being what it was (and is), but we told ourselves it was a test. If we could survive living in one room, we could get through just about anything.

The truth is, in warm weather our living space doubled. Where the apartments below us had a separate bedroom, we had a terrace: a generous piece of open space exposed to sun and air, where we spent most of our time from April to October.

It didn't take long before the urge to grow something took root. We had no clue where to start, but Michael's friend James suggested we try grow-bags. We hadn't the foggiest idea what a grow-bag was, but James made the trip from Massachusetts and set us up. We thought he was a genius, but soon realized how absurdly easy the whole thing is. (Still, props to James for getting us started.) A grow-bag is nothing more than a large plastic bag filled with potting mix and a plant set in it. You grow in the bag!

Grow-bags are perfect for decks and terraces where you can't use permanent boxes (too expensive, too heavy, too large, too permanent). We placed them directly on the ground the first summer in our Pennsylvania house, because we hadn't decided where to put the vegetable garden and didn't want to rush the decision.

Feed Me, Seymour

How often you feed the plants in your grow-bags depends on what kind of soil you use. Topsoil contains more nutrients than lightweight professional potting mix and needs less-frequent feeding. Plus, because you'll be watering topsoil less frequently (remember, it stays wet longer), soil nutrients will be leached away more slowly. A good general rule is to feed plants in potting mix once every 2 weeks, and plants in topsoil once a month.

And here's another great thing about grow-bags: Because you plant new ones each year, you don't have to worry about exhausting the nutrients. Bag the bags and put them out for garbage collection, or, if you have a compost pile, open up the grow-bags at the end of the season, and add their contents to the heap. You'll be surprised by how the plants' roots have filled the bags of soil.

Any way you look at it, grow-bags are an inexpensive, efficient way to start a garden. Whether this is a first attempt or you have a tiny space, whether you have a fear of commitment or just want to be really, really sure of your placement, grow-bags are a perfect solution. I'm warning you — you're going to get hooked.

If you're lucky enough to have access to a roof top, city gardening offers all kinds of possibilities.

Drip Irrigation

Grow-bags make very efficient use of water, as the plastic is nonporous (well, aside from the holes you poke in it) and retains moisture well. A lightweight Pro-Mix dries out more quickly than does a bag of topsoil. You'll have to feel the mix regularly to get an idea of how often you need to water. As the weather gets warmer and the plants get larger, you'll need to water more frequently.

I can't pass up an opportunity to extol the virtues of drip irrigation. Suffice it to say that grow-bags and drip irrigation go together like tomatoes and basil. Because the soil in a grow-bag is enclosed, a gentle rain won't do much to moisten the roots. After you've planted the bags, lay out an irrigation line, with a single dripper positioned at the base of each plant. If you don't have an outdoor faucet, check under your bathroom or kitchen sink. Many apartments have a separate cold-water valve to which you can attach irrigation controls.

If you're using grow-bags on a rooftop, believe me: it's not fun carrying buckets of water up several flights of stairs. A gallon of water weighs 8 pounds, and it takes a lot of gallons to water a garden. The black tarmac of a city roof gets hot, hot, hot, and in mid-July you'll find yourself schlepping water up to the roof every day. Drill a small hole through a window frame to accommodate the quarter-inch tube and let drip irrigation work for you. (For more on drip irrigation, see page 124.)

Beauty's in the Eye of the Beholder . . . Sometimes

If you want a more sophisticated look (maybe the bright-colored writing on the soil bags isn't your idea of beautiful), make your own grow-bags. Use heavy-duty plastic bags, sometimes labeled *contractors' bags.* These should be at least 3 mil thick; 4 or 5 mil is better. (A mil = ¹/₁₀₀₀ inch.) Don't be fooled by the less-expensive, heavy-duty consumer bags. There is *no* *way* these bags will hold up under a full load of wet soil. They'll tear at the first sign of stress and it will be disastrous.

Fill each bag with the growing medium of your choice and tie up the open end. Don't fill the bag chock-full. Use enough soil so the bag lies flat with a soil depth of 4 to 6 inches. Place the bags and proceed as follows.

Plant in Grow-Bags

The fastest and easiest way to go is to buy large bags of potting mix (2 to 3 cubic feet) and plant directly inside them. If you're growing on a deck, use a lightweight, professional mix (such as Pro-Mix) or make your own combo of half Pro-Mix, half potting soil. If you're growing on the ground, you can use topsoil.

The number of plants you can grow in each bag depends on what you're growing. If you want tomatoes, use one bag per plant. Peppers can grow two per bag, and flowering annuals like marigolds, petunias, and zinnias can be spaced 4 to 6 inches apart. Basically, give each plant the same amount of space that you would in a traditional garden plot. You'll find this information on the tag stuck in the plant's pot or on a seed packet.

Use a cutting tool to punch a few holes along the lower edges of the grow-bag, one every 6 inches, and a few more on the bottom of the bag. This will allow excess water to run off.

x marks the spot

Figure out the spacing, then use a permanent marker to mark the spot on the top of the bags where you want the plants to go. Use a sharp knife or box cutter to slice an X on the spot, and fold the flaps back. The Xs should be just large enough to accommodate the root-balls of the young plants.

it's in the bag

Because the potting mix in a grow-bag is lightly packed, the actual planting is quite simple. Just use your hands to move aside enough mix to make room for the root-ball. Insert the plant, then firm the soil around the roots. Continue until everything is planted. Then water well.

An Herb Garden in a Window Box

12

Boo hoo, you don't have a garden. Well, neither do a lot of people, but you don't see *them* buying dried herbs or eating tasteless food! It takes so little space to grow a nice assortment of herbs, there is *no* excuse for not doing it, and you'll have a truly movable feast.

In a 24-inch window box you can easily grow four kinds of herbs, and if your sill will hold a 36-inch box, you can plant half a dozen. Almost all herbs require full sun, so when I said before that there's no excuse for not growing them, I wasn't being entirely honest. Lack of light is a possible excuse, but if you *really* care about fresh herbs, you'll move to a sunnier apartment. Or buy a grow-light (see The Choice is Yours, page 200).

how to   Plant Herbs in a Container

Because a window box usually hangs in place, it's a good idea to use a lightweight container made from plastic or fiberglass. A lightweight potting mix (rather than potting soil) will also help lessen the load. Get yourself a few shards of pottery or some landscape cloth, herbs, and you're ready to go.

A 24-inch box should have three or four, evenly spaced 1-inch drainage holes; a 36-inch box should have five or six holes. Place a pottery shard or piece of landscape cloth over each drainage hole. After covering the holes, spread a layer of potting mix over the bottom of the box. The soil should be deep enough that the herbs sitting on top of it will be planted at the same level which they were growing at originally.

Start with small plants (or, for cilantro, seeds); you can find them at grocery stores, nurseries, and big box stores. Even though you may think you can fit more herbs in your window box, don't crowd them. The plants need space for root growth and to absorb adequate water and nutrition from the soil. Place one herb plant every 6 inches.

special handling

Hold young plants by the root-ball, never by the stem. If the stem breaks, that's the end of the plant; if a leaf is damaged or falls off, the plant will grow new ones.

pop 'em out

You can usually find young herb plants in six packs or 3- or 4-inch pots. To remove them from a six pack, squeeze the sides of the pot and gently push from the bottom until the plant falls out. Catch and support the plant's root-ball in the palm of your other hand.

two for one

Because some herb seeds are fine, the plants may not have been thinned when you purchased them, and more than a single plant may be clustered together in a container. If this is the case, use a sharp knife to cut the root-ball in half and plant each half.

potting up

Space the plants evenly, then fill in around them with potting mix, firming as you go. Don't expose the roots or bury the crown, and leave about an inch between the soil surface and the edge of the window box.

Sweet Basil *(Ocimum basilicum)*

Chives *(Allium schoenoprasum)*

Cilantro *(Coriandrum sativum)*

Lavender *(Lavandula angustifolia)*

What Do You Want to Grow?

Sweet Basil *(Ocimum basilicum)*

Sweet basil is my absolute favorite herb. It just isn't summer without it. All the numerous other types of basil are really just poor relations, in my book. Pretty to look at, perhaps, and useful, I admit, but sweet basil . . . now *there's* an herb worth growing. All basils are annuals.

Chives *(Allium schoenoprasum)*

Chives are a subtle way of working an oniony taste into your cooking. A few snips of the foliage give you a hint of spice without overwhelming your taste buds. The pink flowers have a similar taste and can be broken up to sprinkle into breads and on salads. Chives are a perennial herb (technically a bulb). Zone 3.

Cilantro *(Coriandrum sativum)*

Cilantro is an herb that's fussy about being transplanted. It's delicious, pungent, and well worth growing, but you're better off planting seeds than transplanting small plants. Cilantro is best known for its use in Mexican and Asian cooking. It looks a lot like parsley but tastes way more interesting. Annual.

Lavender *(Lavandula angustifolia)*

Lavender is not traditionally thought of as a culinary herb, but in fact it's a delicious addition to cookies, cakes, and, yes, ice cream! And it smells so wonderful that it's worth growing just so you can rub up against it on a regular basis. There are both annual and perennial lavenders, and many different flower forms. Various zones.

Mint (*Mentha* species)

Mint is absolutely necessary for mojitos, which, contrary to popular belief, should be enjoyed all year long. Unfortunately, mint does not play well with others. If you must grow it (and I must), give it its own container. Otherwise, it will strangle and doom its unwitting neighbors in less than a single growing season. Peppermint, Zone 3; spearmint, Zone 5.

Rosemary (*Rosmarinus officinalis*)

Another pungent beauty, with the bonus of little blue flowers in summer, rosemary comes in two forms: prostrate and upright. The taste is the same, so choose the one whose looks you like most. Zone 7; some cultivars can survive in Zone 6.

Sage (*Salvia* species)

Sage is a perennial herb (hardy to Zone 4) that comes in several colors and color combos: green; green and purple; yellow and green; and green, white, and purple. The plants with more green in the leaves are more vigorous growers, but the variegated plants are more beautiful. Decisions, decisions. Sage dries well, so it's easy to save enough to get you through the winter. Zone 4.

Thyme (*Thymus vulgaris*)

This classic perennial herb grows low to the ground. There are variegated and solid green cultivars, and all are a breeze to dry for winter use. Lemon thyme is especially delicious. Zone 5.

Mint (*Mentha* species)

Rosemary (*Rosmarinus officinalis*)

Sage (*Salvia* species)

Thyme (*Thymus vulgaris*)

Good Neighbor Policy

If you're hanging a window box from an apartment or condo, make sure your building allows this. Strange as it may seem, some places have strict rules about what can be attached to the building and how it must be attached. Heartless, herbless killjoys.

Consider drainage. The excess water has to go somewhere. If the box sits on a sill, average overflow will drip down the side of the building just like rain, but if it hangs from a special holder, great splashes of water may fall onto people on the sidewalk below. It may help to place a tray underneath the box.

Bug Patrol

If your herbs attract insects, you have to choose your weapons carefully (see Knowing the Good Bugs from the Bad Bugs, page 164). You can't use a poison on something you're going to eat. If you pay close attention to your plants, you'll notice insects before they get a foothold. Control small populations by physically removing them or spraying with soap and water.

Ongoing Care

Water the window box until water drips out the bottom. Don't feed the plants for 2 weeks, then feed every other week at half the strength recommended on the fertilizer box. Let the potting mix dry out between waterings. Stick your finger in the mix: if it feels dry an inch below the surface, it's time to water. In a small box and full sun, this could be every day in summer, maybe even twice a day.

In return for a little bit of work, you'll be rewarded with fresh herbs and all the delicious treats you can make with them. How about a Caribbean festival of jerk chicken (using thyme, basil, rosemary, and chives!) and a round of minty mojitos? Top off the meal with some lavender-vanilla ice cream and voilà: an herbal feast from a little plastic box.

Minty Mojitos!

One glass
- 3 mint sprigs
- 2 teaspoons sugar
- ½ lime
- 1½ ounce rum
- Ice
- Club soda

In a mortar and pestle, mash 2 mint sprigs with the sugar. Pour the mint-sugar mix into a glass, squeeze the lime juice into the glass, and add the rum. Fill the glass with ice, then top off with club soda. Stir lightly, garnish with remaining mint sprig, and enjoy!

13

How to Be
Water-Wise

***Xeriscaping* is a fancy word for a simple gardening** principle. Basically, it refers to creating a landscape that uses water sensibly and economically. Originally formulated to help people garden in dry climates, xeriscaping has something to offer almost every gardener. Water is a precious resource and no one should waste it. A few practical guidelines will help you make the most of what you've got, and give you a low-maintenance garden to boot.

Okay, if you don't live in an arid climate, why should you be interested in xeriscaping?

Many cacti make great garden plants.

Sea holly (*Eryngium* sp.)

Weekend gardeners. If you're a weekend gardener, be water-wise by choosing plants that virtually take care of themselves, requiring little supplemental watering. You'll spend less time on garden chores and more time relaxing outdoors. If you work hard all week, do you really want to spend the weekend watering plants?

Picky landlords. Some apartment buildings don't allow tenants to install spigots on terraces, decks, or rooftops. Should the whims of your landlord prevent you from enjoying a small plot of green? Choose plants that need infrequent watering to have a garden despite building restrictions.

Limited resources. Maybe you have neither an irrigation system nor time to hand-water. By selecting *xeriphytic* plants (plants that thrive in dry conditions), you can have a garden that needs very little attention, even in the heat of summer. You'll also reduce the amount of resources (water, food, time, and money) required to keep your garden in good health. Planting with an eye toward drought tolerance makes your life easier.

Container gardening. If you garden in containers, plants are subject to drier conditions than you might think. Soil in containers loses moisture through the planter walls as well as from the soil surface, so it dries out quickly. The sun's heat penetrates the walls of containers and raises the temperature of the soil inside. Roots in a limited volume of soil have less room to search out water and nutrients. Sounds like a xeriscape to me.

Water-Wise Gardening

Here are a few basic principles for planting a water-wise garden:

Shade rules. A spot in the shade can be 20 degrees cooler than a nearby spot in full sun, so put your most drought-tolerant plants in the sunniest parts of the garden. Trellises, arbors, and trees create pockets of shade. Plants that need moister conditions should be located here.

Group therapy. Group plants with similar water requirements. (In other words, don't plant the drought-tolerant yucca next to the water-loving fern.) By doing this, you'll reduce waste and improve your plants' health, since each will receive what it needs: no more, no less.

Right plant, right place. Choose plants suited to your region and micro-climate. Even though a xeriscape in Exeter, New Hampshire, may not qualify as a xeriscape in Santa Fe, New Mexico, it will still conserve resources. Start by looking at plants native to your area; these frequently thrive without supplemental water.

Wholistic gardening. Improve the quality of the soil throughout the *whole* garden bed, rather than piece by piece. This will encourage deep, extensive root growth rather than limit the roots to a small area of amended soil where water and nutrients are in short supply.

Drip irrigation. Drip emitters at the base of each plant can use 30 to 50 percent less water than a sprinkler system. They are highly efficient, delivering water directly to the roots of the plants, minimizing both evaporation and runoff.

Mulch! A 2- to 3-inch layer of mulch cools the soil and helps it retain moisture. Mulch reduces weed growth, and an organic mulch improves the fertility of the soil as it decomposes. It also prevents crusting of the soil surface, allowing water to penetrate to the root zone.

Lean and mean. Don't overfeed. Too much fertilizer promotes weak growth that requires extra water.

Funky Fireplace Planting

Open your mind to the unexpected. My friend Vicky recently moved into a house with a wonderful backyard that featured an old Franklin woodstove. We decided it was the perfect place for a collection of sedums, sempervivums, and other xeric plants. We lined the old grate with a coir (coconut fiber) liner, filled it with potting mix, then planted a variety of hens and chicks (*Sempervivums*). Next, we placed a pot of *Sedum* 'Autumn Joy' next to the stove and plunged a pot of red-leaved stonecrop into the stovepipe opening. There you have it: glowing, fiery colors, without the heat!

Hydrogels

Hydrate the granules before adding them to the soil; otherwise you're in for a rude awakening. I once mixed hydrogels into a container of potting mix, planted it, watered, and left. The next day I got a frantic call from my client: "Ellen, the soil and plants have all fallen out of the window box." Well, of course! The expanded hydrogels had increased the volume of the potting mix at least tenfold and pushed everything out of the container.

That made me look really professional, don't you think?

Creeping juniper (*Juniperus horizontalis*)

Hold the cuts. Keep your pruning to a minimum, as it actually encourages growth.

Weed. Weeds compete with garden plants for water and nutrients. More weeds mean your garden needs more water.

Conditional care. Consider adding a soil conditioner to the garden soil. Water-retaining polymers (aka hydrogels) hold several hundred times their weight in water and release it gradually to the plants' roots; a single teaspoon absorbs a quart of water. Hydrogels can absorb and release water repeatedly. This isn't a permanent fix, although the effects last for 3 to 5 years, depending on your growing conditions. (Fertilizer use speeds up the decomposition of the hydrogels, which is also affected by temperature and moisture.) Manufacturers claim the hydrogels break down into safe, organic compounds (carbon dioxide, water, nitrate, and lactic acid) but there is some controversy about their safety (check the Internet). To date there is no scientific evidence showing this product to be dangerous. Don't breathe in the powdered form, wash your hands after using, and if you want to err on the side of caution, don't use it on edible plants.

Choosing the Right Plants

Certain plant characteristics indicate drought tolerance. For example, silvery foliage and fuzzy leaves reflect sunlight and reduce water evaporation. Succulent plant parts (leaves, stems, roots) store water for drier times.

Even the most drought-tolerant plants need to become established before you can leave them on their own, so don't plant and run. If you plant in spring, water regularly for 3 or 4 weeks, then watch and water carefully for the next few months. If you plant in the heat of summer, you may need to water regularly for 6 to 8 weeks to keep plants healthy. Once a good root system is established, however, a water-wise garden needs little, if any, supplemental water.

Good Xeriscape Plants

Common Name	Botanic Name	USDA Zone	Description
Tarda tulip	*Tulipa tarda*	3	Petit, reliable tulip; yellow and white flowers
Apricot	*Prunus armeniaca*	4	Medium tree; pink flowers, orange fruit
Bearberry	*Arctostaphylos uva-ursi*	3	Evergreen ground cover; white flowers, red berries
Bearded iris	*Iris germanica*	3	24"–36" tall; sword-shaped leaves; large flowers in many colors
Blue mist flower	*Caryopteris* x *clandonensis*	6	4'–5' tall; blue flowers in fall; fragrant foliage
Bougainvillea	*Bougainvillea* hybrids	Annual	Woody vines with thorns; fabulous colors, including magenta, orange, yellow, white, and pink
Brazilian verbena	*Verbena bonariensis*	Annual	24"–30" tall; small purple flowers; basal rosette of foliage
Butterfly weed	*Asclepias tuberosa*	4	12"–36" tall; star-shaped flowers in red, yellow, orange, or white
Common thyme	*Thymus vulgaris*	4	Ground cover; fragrant herb; pink flowers
Creeping juniper	*Juniperus horizontalis*	3	Evergreen conifer; blue berries
Hens and chicks	*Sempervivum tectorum*	2	Ground cover; 2"–4" tall; numerous tight rosettes of succulent foliage
Ivy-leaved geranium	*Pelargonium peltatum*	Annual	Trailing habit; shiny foliage; various flower colors
Lantana	*Lantana* hybrids	Annual	Creeping or shrublike to 36" tall; many color choices; fragrant
Large blue fescue	*Festuca amethystina*	4	12" tall, ornamental grass; blue-green leaves
Mulleins	*Verbascum* species	5	3'–4' tall; fuzzy leaves; spikes of yellow or orange flowers
Pampas grass	*Cortaderia selloana*	8	8'–12' tall; giant grass with showy white plumes
Purple-leaf sand cherry	*Prunus cistena*	2	Small tree; purple leaves, white flowers
Sea holly	*Eryngium* species	5	24" tall; stiff leaves; spiny, silvery flower bracts
Trumpet vine	*Campsis radicans*	5	Vigorous vine with tubular red flowers
Yellow spirea	*Spirea thunbergii*	4	Early white flowers; orange-yellow fall foliage

Plant a Special Bird Garden 14

I have nothing against bird feeders. Really. We put one up every fall in Pennsylvania and take it down every spring. Oh no, wait. That's what we're *supposed* to do. Michael always puts off taking it down because he loves to watch the birds at the dining room window. He leaves it up and then when I'm home *by myself,* the bear comes and rips down the feeder while I stand on the other side of the glass, praying it doesn't realize it could punch

Is it a cottage in the Cotswolds or a bird-house in Boston? Climbing ivy helps camouflage and insulate this birdhouse.

through that window with less effort than it took to rip the feeder off its pulley. This has happened more than once. Other than that, I love bird feeders.

There are, however, other ways to attract birds to your garden. Ways that don't also attract large, omnivorous, marauding, lumbering mammals that cause you to have nightmares about your cat being stolen out of your arms as a snack. But I digress.

If you'd like to encourage birds to visit your yard, you must offer them four things: shelter from predators and the elements, nesting places, water, and food.

Shelter from Predators

A brush pile offers protection from predators and shelter from severe weather. It's also something you can probably put together with materials on hand and it won't cost you a cent.

Choose a spot in the yard that's on the edge of the property, preferably near a tree that offers a canopy. Decide what the footprint of the brush pile will be: Can you give up a 3-foot by 3-foot spot for the purty birdies?

Start with a few heavy limbs (5 to 6 inches in diameter) and crisscross them until the pile is 2 to 3 feet tall. Then poke lighter limbs and branches in and among the bigger stuff, and add a layer on top, 10 to 12 inches high. Finish it off with evergreen boughs. (If you wait to do this step until after Christmas, you can use your cut-up Christmas tree.) The evergreen layer provides protection from snow and rain and keeps the interior of the pile dry. The brush pile should be at least 4 feet tall; the larger you make it, the more shelter it will offer.

Crazy as it may sound, your neighbors may not appreciate the beauty of a brush pile. Some communities have covenants regulating the appearance of your house and yard, so check the rules before starting a brush pile. Even if there are no official rules, you may hear disgruntled murmurings from your less environmentally enlightened neighbors. Do your best to be friendly and reach an equitable compromise. (In other words, don't build the brush pile on your front lawn.) If you can't convince them it's worthwhile, you'll have to choose between the birds and the neighbors. I know which side I'm on.

Nesting Places

The brush pile you construct for shelter can serve double duty providing nesting possiblities for a variety of birds. Some birds make their nests in hedges (robins, sparrows, catbirds) and others prefer to use holes in trees (chickadees, titmice, woodpeckers). You may already be surrounded by hedges and hollow trees, but if you're not, you can encourage birds to nest on your property by providing nesting spots.

The most enticing backyard habitats (from an avian p.o.v.) will have a look of wildness about them. This is not a perfectly pruned garden space, but instead a garden where nature is allowed to work her magic. Leave dead trees standing if they don't pose an immediate threat to people or property. Let fallen, dead trees rot. Not only will birds build nests in tree trunks, but insects and fungi will colonize dead wood and birds feed on these insects, including the dramatically large and impressive piliated woodpecker.

If you don't have space for a brush pile or to leave dead logs on the ground, add a birdhouse or a nesting box or two to the backyard. Place birdhouses away from each other, bird feeders, and high-traffic areas; humans aren't the only animals who appreciate some privacy. Make sure birdhouses are not accessible to predators, including your favorite feline carnivore. Locating birdhouses in the sun will keep them nice and warm.

Water for Drinking and Bathing

Birds will drink from and bathe in the same water source. If you have a water garden or a pond, you're all set. But if not, put in a shallow birdbath. A bath that slopes gently to the center allows birds to walk in to a depth that's comfortable for them: 1 inch for little birds like finches and sparrows and 3 inches for larger birds like robins and blue jays. A birdbath out in the open will enable birds to spot predators who may be staking out the watering hole, and elevating it 3 feet off the ground offers further protection. If

Hollies not only provide shelter and protection (evergreen leaves) but plenty of bird food (lots of berries).

you're really ready to commit, add a submersion heater, which operates on electricity, to keep the water thawed in winter. You can also buy a birdbath with a heating element built into the bottom surface.

Planting Food for the Birds

And now to the dinner menu (I saved the best for last). We're all familiar with the classic robin-pulling-the-worm-out-of-the-lawn pose, of course, but most birds eat seeds *and* insects. When you plant a variety of seed-bearing plants, it's like laying out an all-you-can-eat buffet. A real smorgas-bird!

Many of our favorite ornamental trees offer not only food, but also shelter and nesting spots. Needle evergreens provide important shelter in winter, from wind, cold, and predators. And although I can't in good conscience recommend planting barberry (it spreads like wildfire), I admit it's an excellent food and shelter shrub for many different birds. So if you already have one, leave it in place.

Some herbaceous perennials also produce tasty seeds. If you grow them, you should probably slack off a little on the garden maintenance. You don't want to deadhead too conscientiously because you *want* these plants to set seed to feed the birds.

A Word about Invasives

The longer you garden the more you'll hear about invasive plants. There's a wide range of viewpoints on this, from the native-plants-only tyrant to the wide-eyed flower child who thinks purple loosestrife is a pretty flower. You'll figure out where you stand soon enough.

I love native plants for their history and their appropriate fit with the landscape, and it's true that they're often lower maintenance in their native habitats than exotic imports. But so many exotics are excellent plants it would be criminal to exclude them from a truly mixed border.

It's a balancing act. I don't plant anything so aggressive it will crowd out native plants and the animal life that depends on them. But just because lantana is a noxious thug in Florida doesn't mean I can't grow it in containers overlooking Central Park West. Here are a few absolutes:

✿ **Purple loosestrife** (*Lythrum salicaria*) is a definite no. Don't be seduced by the pretty purple bloom; this plant wants to take over the planet.

✿ **Kudzu.** Ditto for *Pueraria lobata*, except for the purple flower part. Check with local growers or the Web site of Cornell University for a listing of plants considered dangerously invasive in your area (see appendix).

Shrubs and Trees Birds Love

Common Name	Botanical Name	Zone	Growth Habit	Bonus Features
Box elder	*Acer negundo*	2	Tree	Seeds are the primary winter food source for evening grosbeak
Crab apples	*Malus* species	4, but varies with species	Small tree	Boffo spring flowers; humans can share the fruit with the birds
Hawthorne	*Crataegus* species	5	Tree	Ornamental and edible orange-red berries for birds and humans alike
Hollies	*Ilex* species	Various	Shrub or tree	Evergreen species provide winter shelter and protection; edible berries (not for humans!)
Kousa dogwood	*Cornus kousa*	5	Small tree	Large, bright red fruit, tasty to bird and man; ornamental bracts
Mountain ashes	*Sorbus* species	3, 4 (best in cool climates)	Small tree	Ornamental and edible (for birds and humans) orange-red fruit
Red cedar	*Juniperus virginiana*	3	Large tree	Winter shelter and protection; blue berries for bird food
Serviceberries	*Amelanchier* species	4	Shrub or tree	Berries as food for birds and humans
White pine	*Pinus strobus*	4	Tree	Winter protection and nesting; seeds as food
Yew	*Taxus cuspidata*	5	Shrub	Good winter protection

Poking Fun

A brief word about pokeweed *(Phytolacca americana)*. Most people consider this a weed, but I planted one in my garden (as have several of my horticulturally unbalanced friends) because I think it's attractive. You won't find it for sale. Dig up a small one from beside the road; the taproot is unmanageable on older specimens. Many bird species love its purple berries, although they are poisonous to humans.

Being a Good Host

Okay, you're all ready, garden's planted, birdhouses and feeders are set up, water source is established. A few precautions: First be careful with insecticides. A poisoned caterpillar or insect becomes poisoned bird food. Insecticides can also poison a water source. Second, if you've hung a feeder in front of a window (and why wouldn't you?), tack a few strips of reflective foil to the outside window frame, hanging down in front of the pane. Often, a clear window makes birds think there's no glass there and they bash their little heads against it. This can either kill them outright or stun them long enough to make them easy prey as they lie helplessly on the ground.

Birds aren't just endlessly entertaining to watch. They are part of a balanced ecosystem, eating insects that plague man and plant alike. Watching birds also gets kids interested in nature. And don't forget . . . they're purty.

Perennial Plants for the Birds

Common Name	Botanical Name	Zone
Black-eyed Susans	*Rudbeckia* spp. and hybrids	Various
Blanketflower	*Gaillardia* x *grandiflora*	4
Columbines	*Aquilegia* spp. and hybrids	4, 5
Cosmos	*Cosmos bipinnatus*	Annual
Love lies bleeding	*Amaranthus caudatus*	Annual
New England aster	*Aster novae-angliae*	5
Phlox	*Phlox paniculata*	4
Pincushion flower	*Scabiosa caucasica*	4
Purple coneflower	*Echinacea purpurea*	4
Tickseeds	*Coreopsis* species	4

15

Build a
Backyard
Fire Pit

You can't deny the allure of the flame. It's eternal and universal, primitive and irresistible, romantic and exciting. Fire warms all of us no matter who we are; it draws us in. You may find yourself lost in contemplation, listening to the hiss of the wood, watching the flames change from blue to green to yellow. You may wax philosophical, talking late into the night with someone you just met. You may fall asleep with your feet propped against

❖ Burn nothing but firewood! Smokey says burning lawn scraps and cardboard is dangerous, and besides, where's the romance in a cardboard fire?

❖ Keep some kind of fire extinguisher on hand. A few buckets of sand or water will do if you don't have a chemical extinguisher. Don't even think about skipping this step.

❖ Don't use the pit if there's a strong wind. Flying sparks can start a fire way faster than you think.

❖ Don't use lighter fluid or gas. Fire starters that are okay for a fireplace are okay for a fire pit (fatwood and pressed sawdust, for example).

❖ Keep the fire inside the ring. Remember, fire is fun, but it isn't a toy.

the warm stones of a fire pit and the cool breeze blowing across your back, only to have your husband poke you awake and tell you you've been drooling and snoring in front of your friends.

The solstices mark the shortest and longest days of the year, and though a fire is an appropriate celebration for either occasion, a summer solstice fire has more universal appeal. Throughout history, people around the world (Druids, ancient Chinese, early Christians, to name a few) have celebrated the midsummer sun and its life-giving properties. Herbs are thrown on the fire, chants are chanted, music is played, couples couple. I'm getting goosebumps.

In summer, of course, it won't get dark until late, so plan a leisurely dinner, mix a pitcher of sangria and settle in around the fire pit. If the urge comes over you to take off your clothes and dance around the flames, by all means, feel free. But watch out for the mosquitoes.

Anyone can order a portable fire pit from a catalog. Big deal. A stone pit, on the other hand, has substance. It's natural. Face it, it's like Stonehenge: your very own ring of standing stones. You can enjoy a fire pit from all sides, making it the perfect backyard hangout. As the rocks absorb heat from the flames, they radiate it outward. Take off your shoes and rest your feet on the stones; your toes will be warm in no time.

Create a Fire Pit

My husband, Michael MacDonald, has been fascinated by fire for as long as he can remember. He can light a fire in the rain with a single match and make it burn from the outside in or the inside out. Michael not only appreciates the physical requirements of "building the perfect fire," but also waxes eloquent on Promethean philosophy. He calls fire a "mystical dance between air and the earth." Here's Michael's advice on how to build your own fire pit:

First, select a site that's accessible on all sides and is at least ten or fifteen feet from any buildings, trees, and bushes. The overhead space should be completely clear of wires and overhanging tree limbs. Stand exactly where the fire pit will be and look straight up. You should see nothing but sky. Be sure that you've chosen a place free of underground roots. They could catch fire and conduct it along the length of the roots.

Next, dig a round, shallow pit 40 to 50 inches across and no more than 2 inches deep. This will accommodate six to eight people comfortably. Remove all vegetation and pack down the dirt firmly; this will be the base that supports the fire.

choosing the stones

You need something to ring the pit and contain the fire. I prefer stones about the size of a volleyball that have both a flat side and a round one. The flat side faces inward to reflect heat into the center of the pit: the round side faces out. Don't choose stones that have been sitting in or near water. They may have absorbed enough moisture to crack or even explode when heated by the fire.

pack it in

It's okay to pack soil at the base of a stone if it feels wobbly.

16

A Container Water Garden

There's something about water that soothes and inspires, and you shouldn't have to give that up just because you're landlocked. If you have room enough for a barbecue grill, you've got room for a container water garden. Small, yes, but the potential for hypnosis is great.

Start by choosing a watertight container. At the risk of stating the obvious, the container must be nonporous and rustproof. No unglazed clay, no cast iron. You may use a half whiskey barrel (a convenient size), but you'll need to seal the inside. Consider your garden aesthetic

before choosing a container. Which will it be: a large clay pot, glazed a rich cobalt blue, or a galvanized metal trough with an attractive matte finish?

Sun or shade? Place your container before planting. Remember, a pint's a pound the world around (thanks, Mom), so the water garden will be heavy once it's planted. More water plants are available for sunny situations than for shade; thus, if you have a sunny spot, try that first. If all you've got is shade, I'll help you make the best of it.

Perennials or annuals? A small container water garden isn't the best place to overwinter water plants where temperatures drop below freezing. Use annuals if you're going to need to empty your garden after a frost. Think of it as a watery window box, something to plant afresh every spring. Or, if you want to carry over some plants in a dormant state from season to season, you can mix perennials and annuals. If you live in a frost-free climate, well then, the sky's the limit.

Large or small plants? A small container (20 to 36 inches in diameter) can handle three to five plants. Think about the ultimate size of the plants, not how big they are when you buy them. A water lily may be tiny at the nursery, but if it's going to cover the surface of a whiskey barrel when it's mature, you'd better choose something else. Information on plant size should be on the plant tag. If it isn't, ask a helpful and knowledgeable sales associate. I'm sure there's one there, just around the corner.

Preparing a Whiskey Barrel

To make a half-whiskey barrel watertight, apply a liberal, uniform coat of roofing tar with a brush, then allow it to dry for several days in the sun. Or line it with plastic or rubber. You may find a ready-made rigid liner, or make one yourself out of thick plastic (at least 5 mil).

Next, think about how many plants you'll need and what your growing conditions will be. Because you don't have to worry about watering needs (!), you have only a few things to consider:

❖ Sun or shade?

❖ Perennials or annuals?

❖ Size? (It matters.)

My Favorite Water Plants

Black Taro (*Colocasia esculenta*)

Also known as elephant ear, this tropical can be grown as an annual, but it's one that you'll want to overwinter indoors. Each year the plant gets larger, so if you save your tuber for 2 or 3 years, you'll be rewarded with a truly impressive specimen. Full sun intensifies the black of the leaves and the red of the stems, which can be 2 to 3 feet tall, depending on the cultivar. Black taro is quite versatile and also likes boggy and moist soils. Annual.

Cannas (*Canna* hybrids)

You've probably seen these growing as in-ground plants, but they do very well in water gardens, too. Let them start growing in soil, then transfer the potted bulbs to your water garden. Cannas come in a wide assortment of colors and heights. Some have fabulous variegated leaves, others produce flowers in rich, saturated colors: red, orange, pink, yellow. Grow these in full sun and overwinter the dormant bulbs in a frost-free place. Annual.

Chameleon Plant (*Houttuynia cordata* 'Variegata')

This perennial grows in both sun and shade. In full sun, the heart-shaped, green-and-white leaves take on a bright red hue. Chameleon plant can be 8 inches tall, or grow it as a trailer. It spreads quickly, so you may need to divide it at the end of each season, before storing the potted plant over the winter. Zone 4.

Dwarf Cattail (*Typha minima*)

This cattail is the perfect size for a container garden. Slim, swordlike leaves are about 3 feet tall and the classic brown tail stands 1 foot above the foliage. Dwarf cattail grows in full to part sun and should be overwintered in a dormant state or with the pot sunk into the garden bed. Zone 2.

Black Taro (*Colocasia esculenta*)

Cannas (*Canna* hybrids)

Chameleon Plant (*Houttuynia cordata* 'Variegata')

Dwarf Cattail (*Typha minima*)

Golden Creeping Jenny (*Lysimachia nummularia 'Aurea'*)

Horsetails (*Equisetum* species)

Papyrus *(Cyperus alternifolius)*

Golden Creeping Jenny (*Lysimachia nummularia 'Aurea'*)

Here's another garden perennial that does double duty as a water plant. Small, round, chartreuse leaves are grouped tightly along trailing stems and the cascading growth habit looks great draped over the edge of a container. Creeping Jenny grows in sun or shade, but in full sun, foliage color will be more intense and the plant produces yellow flowers. After the first frost, sink the pot into the garden bed, then dig it up and plant it in the water again next year. Zone 3.

Horsetails (*Equisetum* species)

These are primitive plants with a unique growth habit. Slim, hollow, leafless stems can reach 4 to 5 feet tall and are punctuated by horizontal white stripes. They grow well in sun or shade and make an excellent water-garden centerpiece. After a frost, overwinter a perennial species in the garden. Various zones.

Papyrus *(Cyperus alternifolius)*

This tropical is slim and airy, like an ornamental grass topped with umbrella spokes. It grows well in sun or shade and can be overwintered indoors either in a dormant state or as a houseplant, sitting in a bowl of water on a sunny windowsill. Small, greenish white flowers grow on the "spokes," but enjoy this plant for the interesting shape of the stems and leaves. Annual.

Parrot Feather *(Myriophyllum aquaticum)*

The feathery, blue-green foliage of this plant adds interesting texture to your collection. Use it as a floater or keep it in a small pot. It grows to be about 12 inches high in sun or shade. Pot up this plant after the first frost, and keep it dormant over the winter. Zone 6.

Water Hyacinth *(Eichhornia crassipes)*

This tropical plant is an invasive weed in open water and some gardeners believe it should never be used. But it has gorgeous purple flowers and the growth habit is way cool: It's a floater with fat, bulbous stems. Just plop the plant in the water and *voilà*. Plant it fresh every year in either sun or shade; it produces more flowers in sun. Grow as an annual.

Water Lettuce *(Pistia stratiotes)*

Yes, it's another invasive weed, but you should be able to keep it under control in a container. Each plant looks like a mini head of lettuce. This is another floater, no pot required. If it spreads too far, just pull off a piece and give it to a friend. Grow this tropical in full sun as an annual.

Parrot Feather *(Myriophyllum aquaticum)*

Water Hyacinth *(Eichhornia crassipes)*

Water Lettuce *(Pistia stratiotes)*

Plant Your Water Garden

You'll leave most of the plants in their pots within the water garden. Before placing the pots, put bricks or blocks on the bottom of the container to elevate the plants. Measure the difference between the height of each pot and the depth of the water in the container. This tells you how high you'll need to elevate each pot. (For example, if a plant is in a pot 8 inches tall and the water is 18 inches deep, elevate the pot 10 inches so the plant will be at the right level. A small pile of bricks and some basic math will enable you to accomplish this task.

A water garden is the perfect place to experiment with new and unusual plants. Plus, you have the texture and sound of water, the elixir of life without which no gardening would be possible.

it's all relative

Situate the plants according to growth habit and viewing angle. If the water garden is up against a building, place the tallest plant at the back. If the garden will be a centerpiece, viewed from all angles, put the tallest plant in the middle. We put this canna in the middle, because it's going to grow really tall!

cascaders and floaters

Cascading plants and floaters, like the water hyacinths above, should be near the edges. I chose these hyacinths right from the display water garden at the nursery, where they were packed in water-filled plastic bags for transport home.

pump it up

A small fountain within the container brings the sound of moving water to the garden (another nice touch). You'll find small fountain pumps at garden centers and big box stores. These require electricity to operate, so you'll have to have an exterior outlet nearby. Or, try a solar fountain pump. Not only will you not need an electrical outlet, but you'll save money and do a good environmental deed as well. Both pumps are built to be fully submersible.

when summer's over

After the first frost, pull the pots out of the water, drain the container, and cut back the foliage of any plants you want to overwinter.

hibernation time

Put each plant in a plastic bag and store it someplace cool and dark, but above freezing. This forces plants into dormancy until you're ready to plant them again the following spring. Plants that are perennial in your zone can also be overwintered by sinking their pots, up to their rim, into a garden bed.

17

Funky, Recycled Container Gardens

It's a barbecue! It's a container garden! It's a barbecue! It's a container garden! Discarded household junk can bring a little funk into the garden. And who couldn't use that? Nothing lasts forever in our disposable world, but just because your barbecue grill has worn out doesn't mean you have to put it in the recycling bin. You can turn almost any interesting metal container into a planter.

When our red Weber grill began to rust, we replaced it with the super-terrific, bright yellow Homer Simpson model. But what to do with the red one? My gardener friend Mark had the answer. He thought the color of the

Metal doesn't provide a lot of insulation for roots, so in climates with cold winters, use your cast-off barbecue to plant annuals. If you live in a frost-free zone (lucky dog), you can plant a perennial barbecue without worrying that the root-balls will freeze during winter. If you're an argumentative, don't-tell-me-what-I-can-and-cannot-do type of person, go ahead and take a chance. Select perennials that are hardy to at least *two* zones colder than where you live and plant the *center* of the container, leaving at least 4 inches of soil unplanted around the edges (including the bottom) for insulation. Also, leave space between plants, so your perennials have room to grow for at least two seasons.

grill called out for coleus and begonias, leaves of cream and green and red spilling down, poking up, and tumbling out. Clearly, the man is a visionary.

Planting a found item isn't that different from working with other containers, but here are a few special tips:

✿ Make sure there are adequate drainage holes in the bottom. If you're using a cast-off barbecue, á la Mark, there may already be a few. If not, drill or punch out a series of holes at 6-inch intervals. Holes should be ½ to 1 inch in diameter for best results.

✿ Place a layer of screen or landscape cloth over the holes, so you won't lose soil.

✿ Use a lightweight potting mix, not garden soil. Garden soil will be heavy and retain more moisture. Because a metal container is nonporous, the soil will dry out very slowly, and this may speed the rusting process. Also, garden soil is heavy, and this will make moving your container tedious and discouraging. You should have the option of moving your container around the garden, if you so desire. And finally, if it's too heavy, the spindly little legs of the barbecue might snap off, spilling your hard work on the ground, where it will die from exposure or be eaten by squirrels.

As with any other container garden, arrange your plants where you think you want to plant them before actually setting them in place. If you're putting in annuals, go ahead and plant fully, one right next to the other. You don't have to worry about giving the plants room to grow over the next several years, and the container will look more impressively lush if it's chockfull. You'll need to fertilize regularly to compensate for the fact that each plant gets proportionately less nutrition from the smaller amount of soil.

Back away from the barbecue. Have you positioned your plants appropriately? Do you have a thriller, a spiller, and a filler? (See Hanging Baskets: Costume Jewelry of the Garden World, page 28.) Try to envision how big the plants will be when they're fully grown. A 6-inch-tall flowering maple may be 3 feet tall by the end of the summer. Make any necessary adjustments now, then pick up a trowel and approach the target.

Put a layer of potting mix in the container, remove the plants from their

pots, and set them in, firming the mix around each plant. Water the container thoroughly — that is, until water runs out those drainage holes you so intelligently drilled before planting.

Don't fertilize for the first 2 weeks. Allow the plants to settle in and put out a few roots, then begin a feeding program of diluted, water-soluble fertilizer for annuals: half strength every 2 weeks till the end of the summer.

Eventually a barbecue will rust. That's just the way it is, so resign yourself: this is a project you'll start again from scratch every few years. Think of it as an opportunity rather than a limitation.

And by no means are you restricted to barbecues. Plenty of household metal objects can have a second life in your garden: a colander (no drilling required!) of cascading *Calibrachoa*, a wheelbarrow of winsome wishbone flower *(Torenia fournieri)*, an automobile of awe-inspiring angel's trumpet *(Datura metel)*. Please don't make me go on. The point is that by using a funky piece of metal in the garden, you punctuate the scenery in a way that is unexpected, creative, and personal. So give the neighborhood something to talk about and don't be afraid of a little funk.

18

A Dinosaur Garden for Kids of All Ages

In the cool morning mist, ferns bend toward the forest floor, weighed down by morning dew. Springy moss cushions the earth. Suddenly, the silence is broken as the ground shudders. The leaves of a giant cycad shake, then part to reveal a ferocious beast: huge, strong, and armed with terrifying claws and sharp teeth . . . made of sturdy orange plastic.

Is this an excerpt from a grade-B movie? No, it's a scene from your kids' dinosaur garden, full of prehistoric plants and perfect for creative, scary, make-believe.

I firmly advocate getting your little guys hooked on gardening early; you're never too young to play in the

dirt. A child who appreciates growing things will respect the environment, marvel at the wonder of life, and yes, I dare say it, be a better person.

Mom's bed of roses and lavender aren't especially interesting to the juvenile gardener, however, so how about planting a dinosaur garden, with primitive plants that inhabited the earth millions of years ago? Once you've created a prehistoric landscape, leave it to the kids to populate the land that time forgot with an army of T-rexes, velociraptors, and pterosaurs.

Age-Old Plants

Ferns, mosses, and cycads are ancient plants. They predate the flowers and trees we usually have in our gardens, yet they're no more difficult to grow. First, decide where you're going to plant your prehistoric plot.

You can use any of the recommended plants in an outdoor dinosaur garden, but remember, the tropical plants should be considered annuals if you live in a temperate climate. Choose a small plot or set aside a section of your existing garden for the giant plastic lizards. No special soil preparation is necessary; these plants will grow well alongside your regular garden plants.

Four or five horsetails along the back make an excellent prehistoric forest. In front of them, add two or three clumps of Japanese painted fern and a few Christmas ferns. Finally, cover the bare ground with Irish moss or real moss, if you have some available. And for those swimming rubber reptiles, sink an 8-inch cake pan into the soil and fill it with water. Pleisiosaurus will appreciate the effort.

Be sure to leave space in between plants; after all, dinosaurs need room to swing their tails. And no criticism allowed if a leaf gets broken or the moss is trampled. Although you're allowed to help your young gardener with the planting, you don't get a vote when it comes to the garden's plastic inhabitants. These things are best left in the hands of experts.

If you have no outdoor garden space or you think it would be fun to create this project in the family room, do it indoors. Select a container wide enough to allow for serious play. A half whiskey barrel is an excellent choice. Sand any rough edges, then drill five 1-inch holes in the bottom and cover each hole with a large pottery shard or a piece of drywall tape. Next, pour a layer of Styrofoam peanuts into the barrel, 6 to 8 inches deep. (A half barrel full of wet potting mix is very heavy, and plants don't need such a large volume of soil for healthy growth.) Place a layer of landscape cloth on top of the peanuts and staple it to the barrel's walls. This prevents the lightweight Styrofoam from floating up through the potting mix. Next, add a layer of potting soil to the container, several inches deep.

Gather your plants and take a moment to determine the best possible arrangement. Remember, this playground is intended for a very specific population. Start with the biggest plant at the back; a cycad or large rabbit's-foot fern makes an excellent centerpiece. Next, plant a squirrel's-foot fern or a whisk fern on either side, and maybe one more front and center. Finally, fill in the bare spaces with small club mosses for a spongy carpet.

When you're satisfied with the landscape, remove the plants from their pots and set them in, adding more potting mix around the root-ball of each plant and firming it in place. Leave 1 to 2 inches of space between the edge of the container and the top of the soil; otherwise, watering will be a mess. Place the container on top of a saucer or tray, then water well, being sure to wet the entire volume of soil. Stop when you see water run out the bottom of the container into the saucer.

Dinosaur-Appropriate Plants

Christmas fern *(Polysticum acrostichoides)*

A hardy fern with a small, clumping growth habit, Christmas fern is usually evergreen. Dark green, 12-inch-long fronds grow in a low rosette, 6 to 8 inches tall. Part shade and well-drained soil are best for this fern. Zones 3–8.

Christmas fern *(Polysticum acrostichoides)*

Cinnamon fern *(Osmunda cinnamomea)*

Large and dramatic, cinnamon fern grows to 4 feet tall. Each clump of green, upright, featherlike fronds surrounds several cinnamon-colored, spore-bearing fronds at its center. (Young, unfurled green fronds are the classic edible fiddleheads.) It grows well in dappled sunlight and moist soil, but can take full sun if you give it plenty of water. Zones 3–10.

Cinnamon fern *(Osmunda cinnamomea)*

Horsetail *(Equisetum hyemale)*

Irish moss *(Sagina subulata)*

Japanese painted fern
(Athyrium nipponicum var. *pictum)*

Little club moss *(Selaginella kraussiana)*

Horsetail *(Equisetum hyemale)*

This primitive beauty grows well in a wide range of temperatures from tropical to pretty darn cold. It can be invasive in wet conditions, so grow this one in a container or someplace where you can let it run. This is a pencil-straight, evergreen plant that grows 3 to 4 feet tall. It spreads by underground rhizomes to form a dense, forestlike clump, perfect for lurking velociraptors. Zones 3–11.

Irish moss *(Sagina subulata)*

Although this isn't a true moss, it makes an excellent substitute. If you have real moss in your yard, carefully lift a patch by slipping a trowel into the soil about an inch beneath the surface. Plant it in the dinosaur garden by gently pressing the moss sheet onto the soil's surface. If you don't have an available source of moss, try Irish or Scotch moss. Its leaves are chartreuse green and it makes an excellent ground cover, with small white flowers in spring. Grow it in part shade to part sun. Zones 4–9.

Japanese painted fern *(Athyrium nipponicum* var. *pictum)*

This lovely fern is variegated with silver and pink markings. It grows well in shady, moist conditions. Its gently arching fronds (leaves) can be 8 to 12 inches long. Zone 3.

Little club moss *(Selaginella kraussiana)*

Little club moss is a subtropical ground cover that creeps along the soil surface to form loose mats of foliage. Different cultivars have blue-green or chartreuse foliage. It grows best in part to full shade. Zone 7.

Rabbit's-foot fern *(Polypodium aureum)*

Rabbit's-foot fern *(Polypodium aureum)*

Rabbit's-foot fern is well suited to a tropical or indoor dinosaur landscape. Its furry rhizomes are thick and covered with soft, reddish brown scales (that look like rabbit's feet), and its fronds grow almost straight up, reaching 3 to 4 feet in height. Give this fern bright indirect light. Zone 10.

Sago palm *(Cycas revoluta)*

The rigid, glossy, dark green leaves of sago palm grow in a rosette from a brown scaly central trunk. Individual leaves resemble palm fronds, but are stiff and spiky. This tropical plant grows best in full sun. In nature, individual leaves may be 4 to 5 feet long, but in containers they are considerably smaller (1 to 2 feet). Zone 9.

Squirrel's-foot fern *(Davallia fejeensis)*

Squirrel's-foot fern is a tropical fern with lacy fronds and furry rhizomes that creep along the soil's surface. Kids love to stroke the soft "feet" of this plant. New plants are easy to start: use a paperclip to pin a piece of rhizome to the soil surface. It grows best in shady conditions and reaches 10 to 12 inches tall. Zone 9.

Whisk fern *(Psilotum nudum)*

Not really a fern, this odd-looking tropical plant resembles a whisk broom. It has slim, branching stems that grow 12 to 18 inches and does equally well in shade and sun, container and garden bed. It requires moist conditions. Zone 9.

ZZ plant *(Zamioculcas zamiifolia)*

The bright, shiny leaves of ZZ plant are aligned along arching stems that reach 18 to 24 inches tall. This tropical is a very tough plant. It grows well in sun or shade and can survive benign neglect. Zone 9.

Sago palm *(Cycas revoluta)*

Squirrel's-foot fern *(Davallia fejeensis)*

Whisk fern *(Psilotum nudum)*

ZZ plant *(Zamioculcas zamiifolia)*

DOWN &
DIRTY

PLANTS

Vines for Your Garden

19

Psst, show me your vines. Come on, you know you want to. Give me a peek . . . don't be shy.

In the heat of the summer, when vines kick into high gear, all pretense of modesty melts away. These are show-off, hey-everybody-look-at-me plants, and I'm warning you right now: People will want to admire, sniff, and caress your triumphant climbers.

Vines work magic in every garden. They can cover a less-than-beautiful railing, post, or fence. They give you

Will the Vine Eat My House?

Some people fear these plants will damage walls, but please don't be scared off. I grew up in a shingled house covered with Boston ivy and it's still standing, with the original shingles. Here's the deal: If you have a house with brick or masonry walls and the mortar or brick or masonry is at all crumbly, then the vines can speed up the damage. If the integrity of the walls has not been compromised, the vines will attach to but not damage the walls. If your house is shingled or clapboard, the vines *may* insinuate themselves into any large cracks. Again, if the shingles or clapboards aren't cracked, you shouldn't have a problem. Obviously, if you decide to paint or stain, you'll have to pull down the vines and scrape off the traces of stem left behind. If this sounds like too much work, you clearly haven't seen a *Parthenocissus* in all its dramatic glory.

lots of *bam!* without taking up much ground space, and they add height to a garden bed or container. Surely you couldn't ask for anything more.

There are annual vines, perennial vines, vining shrubs, bulbs that vine, flowering vines, vines grown for their impressive foliage, and drought-tolerant vines. Some vines climb via suction cups, others by twisting tendrils, some by roots that grow along the stem, and some simply twine their vines in, out, and around whatever they find. Think about what you like, what you need, and what you've got for growing conditions, then try one of these to get started.

Vines for Fabulous Foliage in Sun

Virginia creeper *(Parthenocissus quinquefolia)* and Boston ivy *(P. tricuspidata)*

These two vines cling as they climb via tiny disks that grow along their stems. Both are deciduous, and before they lose their leaves in fall, their foliage turns bright, bright red. Both grow in sun or shade, but fall color is best in the sun. Virginia creeper, Zone 5, possibly 4; Boston ivy, Zone 4.

Virginia creeper *(Parthenocissus quinquefolia)* **and Boston ivy** *(P. tricuspidata)*

Hops *(Humulus lupulus)*

Not everyone realizes that hops is an excellent ornamental vine. The leaves are large and fuzzy and the flowers are attractive, fragrant, and useful (beer, anyone?). This is a vigorous, twining vine, easily climbing 15 to 20 feet in a season. Try a combination of regular (green leaves) and golden hops (chartreuse leaves) for a swell foliage combo. Only female plants produce usable hops flowers, but don't worry about how to tell the difference. Almost all commercially available hops plants are female. Zone 4.

For Knockout Flowers in Sun

Gloriosa lily *(Gloriosa rothschildiana)*

The King of Bulbs, Brent Heath (co-owner of Brent and Becky's Bulbs in Gloucester, Virginia), sent me some gloriosa lily tubers last year out of the goodness of his heart. Well, that's what he said, but I think he wanted to get me addicted. It worked, and now I'm obsessed with them. In a single season they grow 8 to 10 feet and produce large, bright, spider-shaped flowers. You'll need to start them twining, occasionally tucking a stem where you want it to go. Plant several at the base of a trellis or pole and watch them grow. If you live north of Zone 8 and want to keep your tubers for the next year, you'll have to dig them up after the first frost and before a hard freeze. But oh, it's so worth it. P.S. They attract hummingbirds. Zone 8.

Mandevilla vines (*Mandevilla* hybrids)

This tropical vine makes a great annual climber. Large, trumpet-shaped pink flowers are held among glossy, dark green leaves. This is a twiner that will weave in and out of tree branches or up a trellis all by itself. You can overwinter mandevilla as a houseplant if you have a sunny windowsill. If your plant is too big to fit indoors, cut it back to 8 to 12 inches tall, pot it up, and bring it inside. Annual.

Hops *(Humulus lupulus)*

Gloriosa lily *(Gloriosa rothschildiana)*

Mandevilla vines (*Mandevilla* hybrids)

Passion flower (*Passiflora* species and hybrids)

Climbing hydrangea (*Hydrangea petiolaris*)

Trumpet vine (*Campsis radicans*)

Passion flowers (*Passiflora* species and hybrids)

Passion flower vines cling as they climb with tightly corkscrewed tendrils that grasp any available support. These quick-growing tropical plants make excellent annuals in temperate climates, where they grow well both in the ground and in containers. Their flowers are large and showy with many layers and colors on each bloom. Decorative orange fruit is hollow and not delicious. Annual.

Vine for a Shady Spot

Climbing hydrangea (*Hydrangea petiolaris*)

Try planting a climbing hydrangea at the base of a wall or a fence or even a tree. This vine is actually a shrub (a vining shrub, that is) and climbs via rootlets that grow along its stem. It can grow 20 to 25 feet tall, and won't hurt whatever it climbs on. Flowers resemble those of the lacecap hydrangea: white and delicate, with a flat shape. Climbing hydrangea will grow in full shade but needs an hour or two of sun or bright indirect light in order to flower. Zone 4.

Vine for Tough Conditions

Trumpet vine (*Campsis radicans*)

Trumpet vine can take a lot of abuse. Not that I recommend abusing a plant, but if you have a dry spot, a high-traffic area, maybe someplace that isn't perfectly clean, this may be just the vine for you. Leaves are glossy green and finely dissected; trumpet-shaped flowers are yellow

Fun for Kids

Morning glory. When you're trying to encourage young gardeners, let them plant morning glory seeds (*Ipomoea* hybrids). What could be easier? You plant them right where you want them (no transplanting), they germinate quickly (little waiting), and you don't have to feed them (they bloom better without fertilizer). Morning glories produce copious amounts of gorgeous flowers in blue, purple, pink, white, even stripes! My favorite is the traditional 'Heavenly Blue,' although I'm also fond of cardinal climber *(Ipomoea quamoclit;* photo page 20)*,* a close relative with small red flowers that hummingbirds love. These annual ipomoeas are twiners, grow best in full sun, and do well in containers or in the ground. They can climb all the way up a 20-foot tree in a single summer, covering it with flowers.

Beans. Several bean plants are also decorative vines, growing 10 to 12 feet in a season. Scarlet runner bean *(Phaseolus coccineus)* is covered with abundant small red flowers, and its green pods are edible. Purple hyacinth bean *(Dolichos lablab)* (photo at right) has beautiful, two-tone purple and lavender flowers and shiny purple bean pods (not edible). Its leaves also have a purplish tinge. Both are annuals and grow best in full sun.

or vermilion, depending on the plant. With age, this vine develops a thick, woody trunk and shouldn't be cut back to the ground. The red varieties attract hummingbirds. Zone 4.

Wherever you garden, you ought to have a vine or two. Whether it's a morning glory planted at the base of a curbside tree in New York City or a climbing hydrangea working its way along a shady backyard trellis, these vertical beauties are essential. Without them, no garden is complete.

Homemade Elderflower Champagne

20

I apologize to any oenophiles who will be offended by my casual use of the word *champagne*. I freely admit that this chapter is not about true champagne that is made exclusively from grapes of the champagne region of France. Not that I don't love a nice glass of the classic bubbly, but today I'm talking about a sparkling, barely alcoholic homebrew that slakes a summer thirst like nothing else.

A Little Magic

Pollen of the lacy elderflower is rumored to have magical properties. Hang flowers over your bed at the summer solstice to dream of fairies and elves.

In my neck of the woods, the elders bloom in June. Yours will bloom sooner or later depending on your location, but in general they flower in late spring/early summer. They're easy to spot: flat, lacy clusters of small white flowers on tall shrubs with finely cut foliage.

Don't forage from plants next to a busy road. Heavy metals from car exhaust can make their way from the road to the soil to the plants. Fruits and flowers absorb less than roots and stems, but it's best to pick away from a road, unless it's seldom traveled.

Each 1-gallon batch of elderflower champagne requires six to eight large clusters of flowers. The magic ingredient is the natural yeast in the pollen of the elderflowers. This causes fermentation, which makes the beverage naturally carbonated, occasionally to the point of explosion. But fear not. You will learn from my mistakes and brew in safety.

I've planted two elderberry shrubs in my home garden, to guarantee a supply of the flowers and fruit. (A single shrub can produce enough flowers for several gallons of champagne and still leave some for berries in the fall.) They're most productive in full sun but do grow and flower in part sun. I'd hate to miss out on this yearly ritual. On a warm evening in early summer I crave that homemade bubbly, and once you've tried it, you will too. So stake out your shrubs early, and when the lacy white flowers open, get out there and forage.

Elderflower Champagne

Makes 1 gallon

16 cups water, divided
3 cups sugar
3 lemons, sliced very thin

6–8 large clusters of elderflowers
2 tablespoons cider vinegar

Cooking

1. In a large pot, bring 12 cups of the water to a rolling boil then remove from heat and allow to cool to room temperature.
2. Boil the remaining 4 cups of water in a saucepan, remove from the heat, and dissolve the sugar in it.
3. Pour the resulting syrup into a clean, nonreactive bucket (such as plastic or stainless steel; cast iron is reactive and shouldn't be used for this). Let the syrup cool to room temperature.
4. Add the sliced lemons to the cooled sugar syrup, along with the cooled 12 cups of water, the elderflowers, and the vinegar. Stir it all up, cover loosely, and let ferment without disturbing for 4 to 5 days in a warm spot. The top of the refrigerator is one of the warmest places in most homes and that's where I do this. It's okay to peek if you're curious. You'll notice little bubbles collecting on the floating solids as the brew ferments.

Bottling

1. Rinse, and sterilize four 1-liter soda bottles. Use either a commercial product like One-Step (if you're a homebrewer) or bleach. If you use bleach, pour 2 teaspoons of bleach into each bottle, fill the bottles halfway with water, shake them around a lot, empty, and rinse.
2. After 4 days, strain the fermented liquid through wet muslin (or a jellybag), then pour it into the sterilized bottles. To make it easier for yourself, use a funnel or a pitcher with a good lip to pour off the liquid. Leave a few inches of air space at the top of each bottle and screw on the tops firmly. Squeeze the bottles to get an idea of how much give is in them now. (You'll be comparing this to future squeezes as the bottles harden up.) Store them in a cool dark place for at least a week (in the cellar or at the back of a closet).

Fermenting

1. As the liquid ferments, it produces carbon dioxide, which builds up pressure in the bottles and forces the gas to dissolve in the liquid. The pressurized gas will be released as champagne-like fizzy bubbles when the bottle is opened. Check the bottles every day or so, gently squeezing their sides. You'll notice they get harder each day. When they are rock hard (no give at all beneath your fingers), they're done. Either move them to the refrigerator for immediate consumption (this beverage is best chilled) or keep them in the dark until you're ready. Elderflower champagne will keep for just a few months, so don't wait too long.

Serving

1. Solid particles settle out of the beverage and fall to the bottom of the bottle. Try not to shake the bottle around too much before pouring so as not to stir up the sediment. (It's harmless, but it makes the beverage cloudy.) When it's time to open a bottle, you'll need some patience. There's a lot of carbonation in there, and you'll have to crack the bottle top just a smidge and let it sit in the sink while the gas escapes. Open it too far and the foam will overflow like a bottle of Veuve Clicquot.
2. A strawberry at the bottom of each glass is a lovely touch and gives the drink a festive, pinkish color, perfect for a Fourth of July picnic. (Use one of the berries you flash-froze; see page 55.) But be sure to try a glass plain so you can enjoy the clean, fresh, lemony taste of pure elderflower brew.

Learn from My Mistake

Pressure may continue to build as the bottles sit in the cellar, and here's where it gets tricky. One summer night I was jolted awake, certain I'd heard a very loud noise. Finding no evidence of disaster, I chalked this one up to a dream state and went back to bed. The next day I was looking for something in the cellar and found a sharp shard of thick white plastic on the floor. When I picked it up, I noticed that the floor was sticky. Light dawned and I checked my elderflower champagne bottles. Two of the four had exploded, shattering the plastic bottles and their white screwcaps into pieces.

Now, once the bottles have reached the rock-hard state, I leak a little gas from them once a week — not enough to let out any foam but just a crack so I can hear the gas escape for about 3 seconds. Then I tighten the caps and can once again feel just a little give in the bottles. After a week, the bottles are rock hard again and I repeat the process. Since I've started taking this precaution, I've been explosion-free.

Homemade Elderflower Champagne

Stylish Stakes for Garden Plants

21

I'm not into bondage, but when it comes to plants, I've learned the hard way that they really do appreciate some firm discipline. In early June, it's hard to believe that the stems of your giant black-eyed Susan *(Rudbeckia maxima)* will ever be 6 feet tall, but trust me, they will. You'll be looking at them, wondering if you should do something, then a mosquito will buzz in your ear and you'll get distracted and forget all about it. Until later that night when the skies open up and the rain pours

down. Bombarding those unsupported 6-foot stalks with hard, pounding, constant water. Relentlessly pelting the stately stems until they bend or fall or collapse, without dignity, onto the mulch below.

It won't kill you to take 5 minutes in June to prevent the unnecessary mangling of unprotected plants. Staking is simple and can be either entirely homespun or fancy and high-tech. Either way, the objective is the same: to support your plants in an upright position without detracting from their natural beauty. A good staking job should be almost invisible, undetectable until you get in there among the stems and start poking around.

A Lot of Hoop-la

The growth habit of a plant tells you how it can best be staked. Let's start with peony hoops. Anyone who's ever grown a peony knows that those flowers are super big. Big and heavy. Big and heavy and prone to snapping off *just* before they open in all their scented, ruffled, old-fashioned glory. Pity.

Position peony hoops over your plants early in spring, so that the foliage grows up through the grid. The hidden hoop will support the heavy blooms.

Stylish Stakes for Garden Plants

Place four bamboo stakes around the plant, then loop green garden twine around each stake to surround and support the plant.

A peony hoop is a large metal ring suspended on three or four metal legs, with a grid of metal rods filling the center of the ring, creating open squares 2 to 3 inches in diameter. (There are also peony hoops without the grid, but I find them less effective.)

I can't tell you how often my students have said, "But it's so hard to get all the stems and leaves through those holes!" Well, of course it is. So don't do it. The key to successfully using a peony hoop is to place it flat on the ground over the plant as soon as the peony foliage pokes above soil level; let the supporting legs radiate out from the ring. The stems will grow up through the support grid all by themselves. Once the plant is tall enough (10 or 12 inches), lift the hoop up, carefully keeping the foliage within the grid, and insert the support legs into the soil. Ideally, the grid will be just an inch or two below the heavy blossoms, so choose a hoop height that's right for your plant.

Don't Be Uptight

Always use a tie that allows a plant to grow without damaging stem tissue. This means something stretchy, something adjustable, or something loose. You may use string or fancy Velcro ties, as long as you give the plant some wiggle room. Twist ties are convenient, but the metal strip in the center may cut into the stem of a plant and do serious damage. Loosely tie single stems to the stake with a figure-eight twist.

A Great Deal at Stake

Other clumping plants can be staked with a similar, albeit homemade setup. Many clumping perennials lean outward as they get taller and as flowers mature and become heavy. For this kind of plant (a group that includes coneflower, coreopsis, phlox, balloonflower, and yarrow), use bamboo stakes or gathered branches to establish a perimeter around the clump. Four or five stakes, about 6 inches shorter than the blooming height of the plant, should do the trick. Tie a piece of natural twine to one stake and wrap the clump by winding the twine along the outside of the stakes, pausing to encircle each stake. Tie off the twine when you've completed the circle. If your plant has really floppy stems, you may need more support within the clump: create a pentagram (a star within a circle) by weaving a star pattern inside the circle with the twine.

Staking One by One

Tall, single-stemmed plants like black-eyed Susan, monkshood, delphinium, cosmos, cleome, and foxglove can be individually staked and tied. A general rule for staking is to get it done by the time the plant is a third of its mature height. If you were to sufficiently stake these tall perennials early in the season, you'd have a garden full of 6-foot-tall stakes and 2-foot-tall plants. This would not be beautiful. You have a choice. You can either say, "No way am I doing this work twice," and wait for the plants to grow and hide the stakes, or stake the plants early on with smaller stakes, then redo the job as they grow taller. I won't lie to you; I usually take the easy way out. But you have options.

Either way, *carefully* insert the end of a stake into the ground at the base of a stem. Slide it in as gently as possible so if you meet any resistance, you can stop before damaging the roots. Next, loosely tie the stem to the stake with a figure-eight twist. This will hold the stem more securely than a single loop, but still let it move in the breeze.

Other Staking Styles

Vines can be staked on trellises or arbors, either tied on, or twined in and out of the slats. If you'd like to add vertical interest to a small container, create a tripod of 6-foot stakes. Sink three stakes into the soil around the base of a plant, then tightly bind the tops of the stakes to form a teepee. Your vine may scramble on its own, or you may need to help it get started. (See Vines for Your Garden, page 100.)

Pea staking is an old-fashioned technique used for growing peas. (Imagine that.) It also works well for delicate plants that tend to flop or ramble, like sweet peas, hardy geraniums, and some asters. Collect some leafless branches. Deadwood may be too brittle, so if you're planning on pruning, save some of the leftover, supple branches. Sharpen the cut end of a branch and stick it into the ground behind the plant to be staked. (You may want to use several.) As the plant grows, it will scramble in, out, and between the latticework of the branches.

If your garden is sleek and sophisticated, you'll probably opt for some of the manufactured plant stakes: green, plastic-coated metal in different shapes and sizes. The color is neutral in the plant world and blends well with most landscapes. Some stakes are even adjustable, alleviating the "Should I stake twice or let my stakes dominate the scene?" dilemma.

On the other hand, if your garden has a rustic feel, take a walk in the woods and gather an assortment of fallen sticks and branches. These blend into the background, becoming almost invisible while they do their job. If you're an Ikea kind of gardener, then stick with the natural-colored bamboo. Buy a bundle of 6-foot stakes and cut them to whatever height you need.

Whichever you prefer, be sure you do *something*. Because a master gardener will always give wayward plants the discipline they need.

Provide support for vining plants like this climbing monkshood *(Aconitum hemsleyanum)*, then train young plants by gently winding them around the uprights to encourage them in the direction you want them to grow.

Window Boxes

Maybe you're growing in a window box. If you'd like to add a vine for vertical interest here and if there's a roof above the window box, try this: Screw a series of cup hooks into the roof at 12" intervals. Tie one end of a piece of twine or fishing line to the cup hook and the other end to the railing or windowsill where the window box is located. As the vine grows, direct it up the string to form a curtain of green.

Not-So-Scary Scarecrows

Maybe I'm cynical, but I don't see anything that scary about a scarecrow. Now, I realize I'm not the target audience, but I'd be willing to bet most crows aren't scared either. Well, maybe some rube crow who's a little simple-minded, but your average cawing jackdaw experiences no fear at the sight of the most unusual scarecrow. The truth is, most birds quickly adjust to the presence of a stationary object.

So what? Scarecrows are a welcome addition to any garden, especially if you think outside the pumpkin. Consider this an opportunity to add color and whimsy to your garden, and if you can incorporate some noise and movement, you might actually keep some of the more timid wildlife at bay.

In the United States, bottle trees are most popular in the rural South, where they have been primarily an African-American tradition. The custom of creating bottle trees was recorded in Angola as far back as 1776, and in the Americas in 1791. Slaves captured and transported from Africa to the Americas brought no worldly possessions, but they carried their traditions with them. The popularity of the bottle tree has spread beyond its rural roots, as more people learn to appreciate the eclectic beauty of folk art. I'd like to see one in every yard across the land.

All Bottled Up

My scarecrow is a bottle tree. Back in the olden days, bottle trees were used to ward off bad mojo. Remember the genie in a bottle? People thought if you hung an empty bottle outside the door of your house, you could capture any wandering spirit who came calling. It would be lured into the bottle by the pretty color, then trapped. (Why couldn't Mr. Spirit get out the same way he got in? Maybe Mr. Spirit wasn't very smart.) On windy nights, the bottle moaned as the wind blew over its lip. Or is that a groaning spirit caught inside a bottle? Spooky. A friendlier bottle-tree tradition holds that these bottles contain the spirits of a family's ancestors, which protect a home from harm. Hmmm. So how do they explain the moaning?

You've got options galore when it comes to making a bottle tree. If you have a dead tree or shrub on the edge of your property, simply slide colorful bottles over the ends of its branches. (Kind of an "I meant to do that" way of saying yes, I know the shrub is dead, but so what.) You can also use a large branch or a small tree (dead, of course) with lots of small limbs. Perhaps you like the upright form of a denuded Christmas tree. I chose a gnarled, curving branch from the woods.

Trim the branches to make stubs, 2 to 3 inches long. You'll be slipping the bottles over these stubs, so they can't be wider than the bottle openings.

Find the spot in your garden (or yard) that you think will catch the most evil spirits and dig a hole there. Either plant the branch or tree trunk directly in the soil or set it in a bucket of Quick Crete and bury that. (I tried it without the anchor first, but because I wanted my branch at an angle, it wouldn't stay put and kept tipping closer and closer to the ground. A bucket of Quick Crete and rocks stabilized its position.) Pack the soil in tight around the base of the branch or tree, perhaps reusing the handy 2×4 tamping tool from when you built your own Stonehenge (see page 163).

Next, place your bottles over the branch stubs. Make sure no delicate plants are in harm's way, and put the heaviest bottles near the bottom. It's possible an evil spirit will get ticked off by being imprisoned and shake its way off the bottle tree. I used cobalt blue and bottle-green bottles because

I love those colors together, but the choice is entirely personal. Once you're finished with the bottles, maybe you'll accessorize your bottle tree with some finishing touches. I chose Judy Roger's dancing garden mirrors (see Resources) because I love them. They move in the slightest breeze and the reflections are always changing. Plus I've found they really help keep the deer at bay. And at Jackalope (my favorite Santa Fe, New Mexico, emporium) I found an inexpensive glass wind chime in just the right colors. Some people use long chains of shiny beads or bells.

So now I've got movement, sound, and gorgeous color, and I made it all myself. All thoughts of evil spirits have flown right out of my mind, and let's hope out of the garden as well.

Flash-Banging Noisemakers

If you'd like something equally abstract but less breakable, try the aluminum-pie-plate version. In his book *Scarecrows,* Felder Rushing terms this a "flash-banging noisemaker," which should definitely up the appeal for the little boys in your family.

A collection of different-sized tin pans makes an easy, eclectic scare-whatever.

Forget about It!

Realistic owl and hawk statues are supposed to scare seed-pillaging birds from your newly planted garden. We left one on the porch in the country and immediately noticed the quiet that descended. Hoping to prevent pigeons from nesting under our air conditioner in the city, we took it to New York. The results were not nearly as spectacular. It was quickly covered with bird poop, left as a passing tribute by savvy city pigeons. They weren't fooled for a New York minute.

Collect pie plates and aluminum pans of several shapes and sizes, along with a long bamboo pole (6 to 8 feet) and some brightly colored ribbons. Tie the pie plates onto different lengths of ribbon, then tie the ribbons along the top 3 feet of the bamboo pole. Stick the pole in the ground at a 60 to 80 degree angle, so it bends slightly under the weight of the aluminum. This scare-whatever is perfect for a breezy spot, as the aluminum really dances in the wind and makes noise as the plates bump into each other. And it's a fun, quick project to do with kids. You know what I say about getting them hooked early. (See A Dinosaurs Garden for Kids of All Ages, page 94.)

There are always more traditional scarecrow options, of course, if you're so inclined. Pound a long pole (broomstick size) into the ground and lash to it a shorter piece (shoulder width) at a right angle, about a foot down from the top of the tall pole. An empty bleach bottle or burlap sack makes a face that's easy to decorate with magic markers. Slide the head onto the top of the tall pole, then dress your scarecrow with whatever suits your fancy: an old Bosox cap, long strings of beads, a worn madras plaid workshirt. Does your scarecrow smoke a pipe? Like everything else in your garden, the choice should be entirely personal.

23

Irrigation Systems 101

To irrigate or not to irrigate? I know, you're just getting started and here I am using a technical word like *irrigation*. I don't want to pressure you, but I think you should *start* thinking about this now, for several reasons.

In the past decade, communities across the country have implemented various levels of water restrictions. Even in the usually moist Northeast, several years ago some local governments banned washing your car in the driveway (heaven forbid), and the only way you were

Water is fun, beautiful, and far too precious to waste. Save the hose for cooling down the kids or washing off after a long day in the garden.

allowed to water your garden was with drip irrigation (aka micro-irrigation, aka trickle irrigation). In the arid Southwest, even the use of drip irrigation is regulated.

Not only is drip irrigation extremely efficient and labor saving, but it also improves the health of your plants. Here's how. You go away on vacation in July. You ask your neighbor to water your newly planted tree for fifteen minutes every other day. He promises he will. He doesn't. The tree suffers. If it doesn't die, it languishes. And it's your fault. Or . . . you love to water! Watering is your idea of a good time. Nothing makes you happier than standing in your front yard with a big hose full of *agua*, watering for all the world to see. You love it so much that you way overdo it. The tree roots can't swim, so they drown. The tree dies. If it doesn't die, it languishes. Once again: Your fault. (A plant drowns when the soil is so saturated with water that there's no space left for oxygen between soil particles. Plant roots need both water *and* air, and too much of one means not enough of the other.)

You can set an irrigation system to deliver just the right amount of water at just the right intervals. And if you miss the joys of watering and you have your heart set on performing repetitive, physical labor in the garden, there's always weeding.

When I say consider an irrigation system, I'm not talking about one of those subterranean, pop-up lawn sprinkler systems that go on in the middle of a thunderstorm, spray water forcefully every which way, and are in other ways obviously wasteful. I'm talking about a modest, DIY, drip-irrigation system or soaker hose hooked up to an outdoor faucet, allowing you to deliver the minimum required amount of water directly to a plant's root system. You minimize evaporation loss, maximize efficiency, and cut back on the time you spend on garden chores. Because I spend my days gardening for other people, the last thing I want to do when I get home is work in my own garden. I'm all about low maintenance! A few hours of work in May spent hooking up a soaker hose frees up a lot of time for lounging in the garden with a cool beverage the rest of the summer.

DOWN & DIRTY
ADVENTURES

Fabulous Garden Photographs

24

Tell people you're a gardener and they come at you with the desperate need of a stage mother at an open casting call. Tell them you're a garden photographer and they pull out endless snapshots of out-of-focus daylilies and expect you to kvell.

Even if you're not a professional photographer, chances are you'll want to share images of your garden. Sadly, most garden snapshots don't come close to capturing what the gardener longs to share, primarily because the eye of the camera sees things very differently from the human eye. But if you adjust the way you look at the garden through the camera, you'll vastly improve your garden photographs. And taking better photographs might even make you a better gardener.

The droplets of water on this peacock orchid (*Gladiolus callianthus* 'Karen') lure the photographer in for a close-up.

Why Do You Care?

First and foremost: Focus. When we look at something, we decide what is most important and focus on that. Most of the time we don't even realize we're doing it. If you merely point and shoot with a camera, that personal emphasis is missing. You end up with a broad shot where everything is equal; the result is usually boring and lacking a specific point of view. It's your job, as the photographer, to draw the viewer's attention to the most essential aspects of the scene. There are several techniques that will help you do this.

If you think about *why* you want to take the picture, this will often tell you *how* to take it. Is the light in the garden magical and golden or cool and misty? Has a line of dewdrops collected on the edge of a tight peony bud? Is there a sprinkling of snow on the dried flower head of an ornamental grass? It's not enough to say, "Oh, this is a pretty scene." You need to identify what moves you and what you want to share with others.

This Is a Frame-Up

Once you've answered that question, it's time to frame the shot. If you're enraptured by the dew-bedecked peony, this should be a close-up. From a distance of 5 feet, that magnificent bud is reduced to a little blob of pink against a backdrop of green. So get down on your hands and knees, as near to that flower bud as you can. Show us the soft, velvety, tightly wrapped petals, the reflections in the drops of dew, then we'll understand why you wanted to take this picture.

If you're going for the snow on the grass, pull back slightly to allow for a little something extra. Maybe you'll let us see a piece of gray winter sky behind the dried flower head or some snow on the ground. You're creating a winter scene here, emphasizing the close-up of the dried flower but including specific information about the season. Help us feel the cold.

If the overall ambience of the garden is what you're trying to capture, then you want a wide-angle shot, including a large swath of beautiful landscape. How can you make it personal? Figure out what grabs you most. Is it

A generic, long-distance shot isn't very interesting.

Get down to the tulip's level for an enticing close-up.

the sun's rays slanting through the yellow leaves of a birch in autumn? Is it the impact of a massive planting of woodland primroses? Choose the most important element and give it prominence in the setup.

Point of View (aka P.O.V.)

Once you've decided how to frame a shot (that is, what you will include in the image), select your p.o.v. Walk around the scene, looking at it from different directions. Get creative; consider unusual angles. Lying on your back looking up inside a backlit flower can give you a dramatic image.

Remember those generic (boring) long shots I was cautioning you against? There are a few things you can do to improve their composition. Allow me to introduce you to the rule of thirds. Think of a photo as being divided into thirds, both vertically and horizontally. Place important objects where these lines intersect. Or locate the focal point so that it occupies one-third or two-thirds of the photo. If your shot includes the horizon, don't let the line of the horizon cut through the middle of the frame. Instead, place it along the top- or bottom-third line. If this sounds crazy, try the shot both ways, then see for yourself. I can't explain why, but it makes a much more interesting image.

Light coming through petals of camellia (above) and cosmos (below) highlights their delicacy.

Including a strong diagonal line in the image creates a sense of direction. Is there a path? Place it cutting across the landscape from corner to corner. Turn a square into a diamond by shooting from an unconventional angle. Even something as simple as holding the camera vertically will give you a different perspective.

Let the Sun Shine In — or Not

Lighting is one of the most important aspects of photography. Plants and humans love a bright sunny day, but the best light for garden photography is usually a bright overcast day or a sunny/cloudy mix. An overcast sky (or a large cloud) acts as a diffuser, casting an even light over the scene below. Think Vermeer. In bright sun, the shadows cast by a tree or building are black black black. It is difficult to expose the entire photograph correctly. Do you sacrifice detail in the shadows and overexpose the high light? On an overcast day, you'll capture detail *throughout* the shot. Also, diffused light makes colors look rich and saturated rather than harsh and thin.

The low light of dusk or dawn can be magical. But if you're shooting in low light, you must be extra careful to keep the camera steady. An automatic camera compensates for low light by keeping the lens open for a longer period. If movement occurs (either by the subject or by the photographer)

Bright, direct sun is harsh and creates dark shadows.

Diffuse light makes color look rich and saturated.

while the lens is open, the resulting image will be blurry. To keep things steady, use a tripod or set the camera on something solid: a stone wall, a fence, a chair. Sometimes movement in a photo is an artistic way of communicating intent, but sometimes it's just bad photography. If you blur, make sure it's intentional. And always blur on the side of caution.

Getting at the Composer in You

So now that you know how to take a pretty picture, how does this make you a better gardener? Learning how to compose a shot is a lot like learning how to compose a garden. You'll look beyond an appealing flower and see the bigger picture. How does a background of ferns play off the blue flowers of *Camassia*? Do the yellow flowers of *Corydalis* look better in front of a blue-leaved hosta or among silvery dusty miller? Start thinking about combining shapes, sizes, and colors to compose scenes.

The garden is your canvas and the plants are your paints. Experiment with color and form. The garden is your muse and the camera is your medium. Let yourself be inspired, then capture that inspiration. It's all about developing a visual sense of place and personal style. And showing off the results to friends.

Above left: Snap a shot of a color combination that grabs you, then try it at home in your own garden. (Remember, imitation is the highest form of flattery.)

Above right: The depth of field is narrow in this close-up, allowing the photographer to focus on a single stem of *Scilla* flowers and blur the background flowers for an impressionistic effect.

Container
Gardening
au Naturel

25

No, this project isn't about nude gardening (though I can't deny having done that). In this instance, *au naturel* refers to the container choice, rather than the gardener's state of undress.

You could plant a window box or a flowerpot, or even an old work boot (yes, really) and that would be swell. But think about it: A garden is a representation of nature, right? So why not plant a *natural container* as a garden accent? Planting a natural form punctuates your garden with something surprising and delightful that is also of a piece with the landscape. And it's easier than you might think.

Whether you choose a tree crotch, a stump, or a log, it's best to plant annuals in this kind of container, for several reasons.

❖ The small root-balls of annual plugs are easy to fit into the shallow hollow of a tree crotch or small holes in a log or stump.

❖ The root-balls of perennials require insulation over the winter, and these containers won't provide a lot of warmth.

❖ Annuals allow the gardener to change color schemes from season to season, according to your chromatic whims. Take advantage and experiment.

These plants have been hardened-off and are ready for planting.

Look around your yard and you'll probably find several things that would make excellent containers. Do you have a multistemmed tree? Plant in one or more of its crotches; it's a great way to add a spot of color in an unexpected place.

Maybe you have a tree stump that sits there accusingly, reminding you to call the stump-grinder guy or get out some truly toxic chemicals to dissolve the remaining wood into nothingness. Put down that bottle of Stump-Away! and pick up a drill instead. By making a large-diameter hole in the top of the stump, you can use it as you would a pot.

Do you have fallen logs at the edges of your garden? When a tree falls, there's often some rot going on, which means the wood is soft and easy to work with. Poke along the length of the log, looking for a soft spot, and pull out any rotted wood until you have a hollow large enough to plant. You may need to use a hammer and chisel, but it's entirely possible to find a nicely rotted log just waiting to be planted.

Got rock? If you're short on wood, there's always stone. A boulder with a shallow hollow on top can be planted with an annual succulent like portulaca or ice plant *(Mesembryanthemum)*. If the hollow is a few inches deep, you can plant super-hardy perennial succulents like hens and chicks or stonecrop. When planting succulents, use a soilless potting mix instead of potting soil. It will drain more quickly and allow the roots to dry out between waterings.

No flat boulders? Consider gathering a few upright stones to create a bottomless container: a small, tight circle of standing stones. The stone container may be small (holding a few impatiens or a single fern) or large, depending on the number of rocks in your garden and the strength of your back and biceps.

Any garden feels more serene and welcoming when it fits, not fights, its surroundings. A collection of ferns and mountain laurel would be jarring in Arizona but fits perfectly in Vermont. Look just beyond your fence or deck for inspiration on how to make the most of what you've got.

Plant in a Hollow Log

Fill your container with potting soil, then arrange your annuals the way you want them, before taking them out of their pots. Plant a few trailers near the front, to cascade downward. A vining annual like a tender ivy or creeping fig will root along the bark, covering the surface with foliage. Place something upright at the back for a focal point. If you're planting the crotch of a tree, consider a fast-climbing vine like morning glory or passionflower. These will scramble up a trunk and weave among the leaves over the course of a summer, adding tremendous vertical interest. And don't worry, the roots of annual vines won't hurt the tree!

Most natural containers aren't huge, so a combination of two or three plants is more than enough. Too many competing colors and shapes will be discombobulating, which is not usually an effect we strive for in the garden. Try something thematic: various shades of blue flowers, flowers with silvery leaves, plants with variegated foliage, for instance.

Planting a natural container is a great way to harmonize your garden with the surrounding landscape, blurring the lines between cultivation and unadulterated nature. It also lets you add spots of color in places where a pot or box would be impractical or out of place. Try a little container gardening *au naturel*, enjoying nature in all its naked glory.

add potting soil

Fill the hole or hollow with potting soil. You don't need to worry about drainage holes, because excess water will run out of a tree crotch, be absorbed by the bark, or escape through cracks in wood or stone and holes in a stump or log. Porous wood also allows moisture to evaporate through the sides of the container.

fix 'em pretty

Play with the plants before taking them out of their pots: trailers to the front where they can cascade downward; taller plants as focal points at the back.

settle in

Remove the plants from their containers, scoop out a place in the potting soil so that they'll sit at the same level they grew at in the pot, and set them in place. Add more soil around them and press them firmly into their places.

A Garden to Delight Your Senses

26

People smell plants, they gaze upon them in admiration, they even eat them. But how many stop to brush up against the sensuous surface of a fuzzy leaf or rub the leaves of a fragrant herb between their fingers, releasing the essential oils? Not many people caress their plants the way they should. It's time for that to change.

Plants are touchable for lots of reasons. Some are soft, some are fragrant, some are smooth and succulent, some are sharp and pointy but, nevertheless, irresistible. Plant a touching garden near a door or entryway so you can reach down as you pass and enjoy the textures and fragrances at hand.

Clary sage *(Salvia sclarea)*

Lamb's ear *(Stachys byzantina)*

Solanum *(Solanum pyracanthum)*

Stonecrop *(Sedum seiboldii)*

Touchable Plants

Clary sage *(Salvia sclarea)*

This biennial herb has huge, fuzzy leaves and spikes of white flowers. A rosette of foliage can be 18–30 inches wide and 12 inches tall; the bloom spike may be 24–30 inches tall. The large, white, hairy leaves cry out to be caressed. Zones 5 and 6.

Lamb's ear *(Stachys byzantina)*

Kids are constantly being told not to touch, so why not plant something especially for them to play with? No child can resist lamb's ear. It begs to be brushed softly against your cheek or hand. The leaf surface is furry and white, eminently touchable. And it's a great garden plant to boot. Grow it in full sun as a ground cover at the front of your touching garden. Zone 4.

Solanum *(Solanum pyracanthum)*

Not everybody considers *Solanum pyracanthum* a touchable plant, but I like to encourage personal eccentricities in the garden. This plant grows best in full sun and will reach 18 to 24 inches tall. It's spiky and weird-looking, with orange midribs, ferocious orange thorns on those midribs, and purple flowers. Deer don't touch it — one look at the half-inch thorns will tell you why. And yet I can't keep my hands off these plants. Gently press the pad of your index finger against the tip of a thorn. The risk of pain and injury gives you a little thrill, doesn't it? Do this only if you're over the age of 18. Children should not be allowed to play with thorny solanums. Annual.

Stonecrop (Sedum seiboldii)

If you prefer fleshy to fuzzy, how about a plump, smooth stonecrop? This ground cover has circular, gray-green leaves and clusters of pink flowers at the end of each stem. The leaves are turgid (firm and plump), and squeezable, and surprisingly cool to the touch. Zones 4 and 5.

Aromatic Plants

Lavender (Lavandula angustifolia)

Lavender has it all: small silvery leaves, pretty lavender flowers, and a smell that both relaxes and exhilarates. It can never become mundane because it's just so damn good. Lavender grows to be 12 to 24 inches tall, depending on the variety. Zone 5.

Rosemary (Rosmarinus officinalis)

Another highly fragrant herb, rosemary is wonderful for cooking. But we're talking aroma here. Squeeze your rosemary to release essential oils that will make your fingers smell edible. Zone 6–8, depending on the variety.

Santolina (Santolina chamaecyparissus)

This herb has very finely cut, silver foliage and yellow, buttonlike flowers. It gets to be 8 to 12 inches tall and is intensely fragrant. Zones 6 and 7.

Scented geraniums (Pelargonium species)

You can grow scented geraniums as garden annuals or as houseplants. Or both. There are dozens of scents: lemon, chocolate, and nutmeg, to name a few. Rub the foliage to release essential oils, and enjoy the felty leaf surface.

Lavender (Lavandula angustifolia)

Rosemary (Rosmarinus officinalis)

Santolina (Santolina chamaecyparissus)

Scented geraniums (Pelargonium species)

Community Begins with a Community Garden

There wouldn't be so many gardeners out there if gardening didn't *do* something for us; not just feed us and give us beautiful landscapes to admire, but also satisfy something within — an urge to nurture, create, produce, work with (not struggle against) the land. Getting dirty isn't always a bad thing. It depends on how you do it.

Look at any big city: concrete sidewalks, polluting traffic, litter on the streets, garbage dumped in vacant lots. And community gardens. You don't see them? Look more closely; they're there.

Boston's Fenway Victory Gardens are the last remaining original victory gardens in the United States. They were started during World War II to help alleviate food rationing.

Sometimes community gardens are large and well-organized sprawls, sometimes they're narrow lots taken over by gardening guerrillas who've claimed squatting rights. Community gardens unite a group of people who want to garden but don't have their own space. Sometimes community gardeners are those who need more space. (It's not easy to grow tomatoes in a shady Brooklyn backyard.)

Community gardening is a panacea. It's a catalyst for neighborhood development and interaction. It beautifies a neighborhood and helps families trim their food budget by enabling them to grow fresh vegetables. Community gardening teaches participants about conserving resources and treasuring the environment, and it gets people moving, providing physical activity. I will go so far as to say that a community garden embodies the very essence of community: inclusive, unifying, and stimulating.

You find every kind of community garden in a big city. Unofficial sites exist under constant threat of being bulldozed, but many persist nonetheless. Sometimes a plot begun by a group of squatters ends up as a protected site, granted official sanction for use for long periods of time. Sometimes they're destroyed, replaced by a parking lot or high-rise condos. But it's difficult to defeat gardeners. (Gardening is optimistic by nature. Why plant a seed if you don't believe it will grow?) Even a heartbroken community gardener will heal, and soon be digging in another spot.

Join In

If you'd like to join an existing community garden, take a walk in your neighborhood. Is there a local group with an empty plot? Maybe you can put your name on the waiting list for next year. Or check the Web site of the American Community Gardening Association (ACGA). (See appendix.) This is an excellent, comprehensive site, and includes an organized list of existing community gardens across the United States and Canada, along with links to local organizations. You can also check with the nearest Cooperative Extension office for community gardens in your area.

Community garden groups are structured in different ways. In some, you pay annual dues, and the money goes toward general garden maintenance and supplies. In others, you promise a number of hours of work in the common areas (maintaining paths, turning compost piles, repairing tools and hoses, for example). Some gardens are structured around a specific group, like families, the elderly, or children. Groups run the gamut from highly structured and organized to loosey-goosey. Find one that fits your modus operandi. It's an excellent way to improve your gardening skills. Fellow gardeners will be eager to share their expertise; in fact, they probably won't be able to contain their enthusiasm.

Community gardens include a wide variety of garden styles, and community gardeners come in all types and ages!

Start-up

If by some chance there's no community garden in your neighborhood, perhaps you'll be so bold as to start one with a group of like-minded individuals. Again, the ACGA is an invaluable resource. A lot of its information is available free of charge on its Web site, but splurge on a membership if you can. It's inexpensive, and then you can devour all its most excellent information. Here are a few basics to consider before starting a community garden.

Community gardens usually have rules about maintaining individual plots.

Sunny-side up. Most community gardeners want to grow vegetables, or maybe a vegetable/flower combo. Few set out to cultivate hostas and ferns. Look for a site that gets at least 6 hours of sun per day. In densely populated urban areas, building shadows block available rays, so be sure to check.

Safe soil. Do a soil test before making a commitment (like checking out a new babysitter before leaving her alone with the kids). Because you'll be growing edible plants, it's important to check for heavy metals and other soil contaminants.

Watering wisely. Where's the closest available water? Wherever you garden, there are times during the growing season when you'll have to water. How far are you willing to haul H_2O? What are the chances of installing basic plumbing on the site?

Storing things. Is there room for a community storage shed? Individual members may have space in the shed, or use it for jointly owned equipment. A slightly larger community space can be an impromptu community center, giving people a place to relax and socialize after a hot afternoon in the garden.

Plant a Row

Plant a Row (also known as PAR) is a group with affiliates in the United States and Canada that encourages gardeners to grow an extra row of food for donation to local food banks. If you can't manage an extra row, how about an extra plant or two? PAR connects gardeners to local groups that distribute the food to those in need, and the results have been remarkable. Since 1995 they've collected and distributed more than 8,000,000 pounds of food grown by thousands of volunteers.

What easier way could there be to volunteer than to grow a little extra food in a community garden plot? You're already out there digging and watering and weeding anyway. For information on how to hook up with PAR, including suggestions about which vegetables are easiest to pack and ship, and how to get in touch with local distribution networks, see Resources in the appendix.

Leases. Sometimes you can get a lease, sometimes you can't, but it's always a good idea to try. Look for an initial commitment of 3 to 5 years. This gives you time to work out the bugs(!) and establish the garden as a neighborhood asset.

And . . . Other things to consider are wheelchair accessibility, membership fees, and plot size. Yes, it's a lot to think about, but not all of it has to be worked out from the beginning.

If you're a type-A personality, you may find yourself drafting a mission statement before you even break ground. But it's equally possible for a group to coalesce naturally around a love of fresh vegetables. You shouldn't have to give up the delights of a sun-warmed tomato just because you live in downtown Chicago.

Building More Than Just Gardens

Let's take this community-building thing one step further. Some community gardens are begun in response to a community crisis. Bissel Gardens in the Bronx, for example, was created in an effort to take back the streets of a neighborhood that was quickly becoming unsafe. Now it covers more than 2 acres of land (flush up against some elevated train tracks) and consists of individual garden plots, jointly farmed plots that grow fresh vegetables for local soup kitchens, and a small nursery where trees and shrubs are grown for city parks. In come the gardeners, out goes urban blight.

We can't all be land barons, but we can all learn to garden. Doing that as part of a community brings a wonderful sense of sharing to an already satisfying occupation. Each of us can grow a few fresh vegetables and herbs for ourselves, our families, and maybe even a little extra to share. Community begins with a community garden.

28

Coexisting with Bambi

Don't get me started. Yes, I read *Bambi*. Yes, I cried when Bambi's mother was shot. (No, I didn't see the movie. My mother thought it would upset me.) To be honest, I have nothing against deer, as long as they stay out of my garden.

The truth is, the deer were there first. We're moving into their territory as sure as we're encroaching on the habitats of many other creatures great and small. A deer's life depends on eating our plants way more than our lives depend on them not eating our plants.

Now I've had cats and I've had dogs and neither needs as much supervision in the garden as my nephew Nate. Dogs and cats seem to instinctively know which plants to avoid — perhaps they attend the same school the deer do. On Natey's first visit to our house in Pennsylvania, he made a beeline for the poisonous berries and popped one in his mouth. Being possessed of catlike reflexes, I reached in and grabbed the berry before he could swallow, but this taught me a valuable lesson.

Some kids are nibblers and some aren't; I'm sure you know which you've got. If your children tend to put things in their mouths, do *not* plant poisonous plants. That may seem obvious, but let's not take any chances here. You'll just have to put up with deer damage until your kids grow out of their nibbling stage.

So, can we coexist peacefully with Bambi? Yes, but the burden is entirely on us. To date, I've had no luck convincing the deer population in northeastern Pennsylvania that compromise is worthwhile. Therefore, I suggest a multipronged, deer-discouraging approach.

The best thing you can do is plant unappetizing (but beautiful) plants in your garden. Now, you're going to see a lot of different lists with a lot of different plants touted as deer resistant. Let me tell you right now that none of these lists is gospel. Why? Because deer don't eat the same things all the time. Appetites vary with location and time of year, and deer that live someplace with lots of food to choose from may avoid some plants in favor of others. In areas with a high deer population and not much food, however, they'll eat just about anything to stay alive.

So I say, "Focus on the poisonous." No, not to kill them, just to discourage them from eating at your restaurant. I occasionally (and briefly) wonder how a deer (or any other animal) knows that a plant is poisonous. Does the herd pool its vast accumulation of plant lore, then conduct classes? Do poisonous plants emit a special scent that telegraphs an invisible warning? Do deer try the plant once, feel sick, and learn a lesson? Or do young deer watch what their elders are eating and simply copy them? Don't know. Don't really care. All I can tell you is that the truly madly deeply poisonous plants don't get eaten.

Not a Tasty Menu

Angel's Trumpet *(Brugmansia)* and Devil's Trumpet *(Datura)*
All parts of these plants are heavy-duty psychoactives — in other words, extremely poisonous. Both are tropical plants, but you can grow them as garden annuals in a temperate climate. Flowers are fragrant, large, and trumpet-shaped. Generally speaking, angel's trumpet flowers hang down; the flowers of devil's trumpet point up, or are horizontal. Colors range from soft pastels to rich shades of purple and orange. Annual.

Devil's trumpet (*Datura*)

Bugbane *(Actaea racemosa 'Atropurpurea')*

Bugbane *(Actaea simplex, A. racemosa)*

These are shade plants, but they'll take sun if you give them plenty of water. The leaves are finely cut; flowers are white and shaped like bottle brushes. Bugbanes attract lots of pollinating bees to the garden. Some cultivars have reddish purple foliage. A close cousin of bugbane is doll's-eyes *(Actaea pachypoda,* Zone 4). The ripe berries of doll's-eyes are pure white with a black dot in the middle, hence its common name. Grow it if you don't mind being stared at while you garden. *A. simplex,* Zone 4; *A. racemosa,* Zone 3.

Daffodils (*Narcissus* species and hybrids)

We all love spring bulbs; they perk us up just when we need it most, and I'm not talking about four o'clock in the afternoon when all we really need is a piece of chocolate to get us over the hump. Daffodils are *never* eaten (not the flowers, not the foliage, not the bulbs) because they are poisonous. Tulips, on the other hand, are considered tasty by deer and chipmunks alike. (And a host of others besides: Did you know the Dutch ate tulip bulbs during World War II?) Various zones.

Daffodils (*Narcissus* species and hybrids)

Foxglove *(Digitalis purpurea)*

Lily of the Valley *(Convallaria majalis)*

May Apple *(Podophyllum peltatum)*

Foxglove *(Digitalis purpurea)*

This plant contains chemicals that work on the heart; the drug digitalis was originally derived from foxglove. However, if you're *not* experiencing congestive heart failure, the effects from ingesting are bad. A biennial plant, foxglove bears tall spikes of bell-shaped flowers of pink, cream, purplish, or yellow, all dappled with brown spots. It grows best in part sun and reaches 3 to 6 feet in height. Zone 3.

Lily of the Valley *(Convallaria majalis)*

How can such a pretty, delicate white flower with such a sweet scent be such a strong and deadly poison? Ah, the mysteries of life. Lily of the valley contains cardiac glycosides that are *muy peligroso* to humans and animals alike. These shade plants spread rapidly. Zone 2.

May Apple *(Podophyllum peltatum)*

This native North American plant is a woodland wildflower that also does very well in shady gardens. I've been seeing it at nurseries more and more frequently, and hope more people will grow it. Two large, deeply lobed leaves are held horizontally, looking like large umbrellas. A single yellow and white flower is borne beneath the leaves and is followed by the fruit, which is the only part of this plant that isn't poisonous. Zone 4.

Milkweed *(Asclepias syriaca)*

Considered a weed by some, milkweed spreads rapidly via underground stems. I pull up about half of the volunteers and leave the rest in the garden, where they are both ornamental and poisonous. Milkweed grows to about 3 feet tall and has numerous clusters (umbels) of pink and purple star-shaped flowers. They grow best in full sun and are drought tolerant, due to their long taproot. Zone 3.

Monkshood *(Aconitum napellus, A. carmichaelii)*

I'd love monkshood even if it weren't 100 percent deer-proof. These tall perennials (3 to 5 feet) are perfect for the back of the border. They grow well in shade or sun but require extra water in sites with more light. Leaves are deeply lobed and the stems are strong and upright. (Stake them anyway, just in case there's a late-summer deluge.) Flowers are borne in spikes about a foot long; they are deep blue-purple, a lovely, rich, cool color. Zone 3.

Bane of Your Existence

Another common name for monkshood is *wolfbane,* so called because it was thought to poison wolves back in the days when wolf poisoning was in vogue. Pretty much any plant with the word *bane* in it is poisonous. And that's a good indication it won't be eaten by deer.

Milkweed *(Asclepias syriaca)*

Monkshood *(Aconitum carmichaelii)*

Poppies (*Papaver* species)

Poppies (*Papaver* species)

We've all seen *The Wizard of Oz,* right? Remember when Dorothy and her pals fell asleep in the poppy field? Opium comes from *Papaver somniferum* (illegal to grow in the United States, Canada, and many other countries), but other (legal) poppy species produce similar chemicals that are poisonous to humans and animals. There are both annual and perennial poppy species. All grow best in full sun, where they produce delicate, crepe-papery blooms in a wide variety of rich colors: oranges, pinks, reds, and maroons. Various zones.

Rhubarb *(Rheum rhabarbarum)*

Rhubarb *(Rheum rhabarbarum)*

"But wait a minute," you're thinking. "We *eat* rhubarb, so how can it be poisonous?" Here's the scoop: We eat the petioles (leaf stems), which are tart but safe. The leaves, however, are poisonous to people and livestock (and deer). Rhubarb is not only an excellent edible plant, but it's also quite attractive with its red stems and large leaves. Grow it in full sun and give it plenty of space; the plant can reach 5 feet wide. Zone 4.

Try and Try Again

I promised you a multipronged approach and a multipronged approach you shall have. There are a few things you can do to discourage browsing in addition to planting unappetizing plants.

Fencing. This may seem like an obvious solution, but deer are prodigious jumpers. A single fence has to be 10 feet tall. A double fence (one fence set 4

Nonpoisonous Deer-Resistant Plants

❖ **Ornamental grasses** have very sharp edges, which deer tend to avoid.

❖ **Fuzzy-leafed plants,** like lamb's ears and verbascums, are also unappealing. My (I admit, slightly wacky) theory is that the texture of the leaves feels like fur to them, and deer are vegans.

❖ **Extra-thorny plants** are also usually safe, but the thorns have to be truly threatening, like those of hardy orange (*Poncirus trifoliata*). Itty-bitty rose thorns mean nothing to the peckish deer.

This works as well as the store-bought sprays based on putrescent egg solids. Whisk one egg with a good squirt of dishwashing liquid and a tablespoon of garlic powder. Pour into a 2-gallon sprayer and add 2 gallons of water. Mix, pump, and spray. Apply a thin coat, let dry (10–15 minutes), then apply another thin coat. To keep new growth protected, reapply every 2 weeks or after a heavy rain.

feet inside of the other) can be 6 feet tall. An electric fence is also effective and should consist of two strands: one at 18 inches and one at 4 feet. Having survived several close encounters with an electric fence, I can say with certainty that although it doesn't kill you, it's an excellent deterrent.

Scent. Deer have extremely sensitive noses; scents we humans can barely detect are quite strong to deer. In many instances, a strongly scented plant will deter browsing just by virtue of its aroma. Deer rarely eat strong herbs like lavender, oregano, and rosemary. We can use disgusting smells to keep deer out of garden beds. Many commercial sprays are composed of putrid egg solids and water. The smell is barely noticeable to humans once the spray has dried. It needs to be reapplied after a heavy rain or every 2 weeks.

Milorganite (a fertilizer made from processed sewage) is not sold as a deer deterrent but works quite well for me. I place piles about 2 inches high at 3-foot intervals around a garden bed. I don't apply it at the base of plants at this intense concentration, because it could damage plant tissue. When Milorganite is used as a fertilizer, it's used in much lower concentrations.

Deervik. This new product is a yucky, pasty substance that you apply to a stick or tag, which you then hang on a plant or stick into the soil near the plant's base. It's effective for several months, won't wash off in the rain, and, though the paste smells bad close-up, it's not noticeable (to our human noses) from a distance of 2 or 3 feet.

So go ahead and appreciate wildlife all you want, but don't be afraid to set some boundaries. Bambi is always cuter on the other side of the fence.

Don't Try These at Home

There are so many things that *don't* work to deter deer. Let me save you some time and money. Don't bother with: bags of hair hung on trees, soap hung on trees, motion sensor–activated water sprays and ultrasonic screamers, coyote urine, or hot pepper spray. The hair and soap just don't work and I don't know why anyone thought they would. The motion-sensor devices work the first few times, but deer learn very quickly that there are no real consequences and keep on eating. The predator urine smells hideous, and there's some controversy over whether it's truly predator urine. The hot pepper spray is not effective. These opinions are from my own experiences and I suppose things might be different for you. But I doubt it.

Growing (and Eating!) Blueberries

People compete to be our weekend guests in July. It has nothing to do with our charming company and only a little to do with the pure, spring-fed waters of Twin Lakes. They come for the blueberries.

Blueberries are a great fruit crop to try at home: They don't take up much space, a few good-sized bushes give you enough berries to actually make something with, and you don't have to wait too long for the plants to mature and bear fruit. Plus, in addition to tasty fruit, they produce dainty, white, bell-shaped flowers in spring and flaming red foliage in fall. Three seasons of interest in one plant!

The Worldwide Soil Food Web

Soil food web expert and my pal Jeff Lowenfels (author of *Teaming with Microbes*) says, "If you're an organic or natural gardener, then to acidify your soil you need to stimulate fungal activity, primarily decay. Brown mulches like autumn leaves, kelp meal, and bark chips all promote fungal growth and should be placed on the soil to at least the plants' driplines. Pine needles are also a good mulch provided they have aged. Don't use green mulches like grass clippings, straw, hay, alfalfa, and blood meals. These promote bacterial activity which tends to increase the alkalinity of the soil."

Blueberries grow best in full sun and like a moist, well-drained soil, so choose a spot with these conditions. If your soil is heavy clay, consider growing blueberries in a raised bed to improve drainage.

The Acid Test

Blueberries need acid soil. If azaleas and rhododendrons thrive in your garden, so will blueberries. Test the soil where you want to grow the berries. (For advice about acid soil and soil testing, see It Ain't Just Dirt, pages 216-221.)

✿ If the soil pH is higher than 6.0, or if you garden on a terrace or deck, try blueberries in a container. A half whiskey barrel is a good size for a single bush. Use a soilless mix, which is generally acidic, and feed with a fertilizer high in nitrogen.

✿ If the soil acidity is between 4.0 and 4.5, do nothing; you're good to go.

✿ If the soil pH is between 4.5 and 6.0, you'll have to amend it. Granulated sulfur is the traditional solution, but may form sulfuric acid when combined with water. This can kill important soil microorganisms. Instead, add a naturally acidic material: composted leaves, pine needles, sawdust, or cypress bark. You'll need 4–5 gallons per bush.

Outline your "blueberry bed," allowing 2 to 3 feet for each bush. Finely chop the acidic organic material, then spread it on top of the bed. Now, dig it into the soil to a depth of about 8 inches. The resulting soil mix in this newly prepared bed should be about half amendments and half garden soil. Now your soil is ready to plant.

Setting in the Plants

Blueberries require excellent drainage. To provide it, plant the bush so that the crown of the shrub is 2 to 3 inches above the soil line. I know, I know, I told you never to do this and now I'm contradicting myself! I promise, in this particular instance, it's okay to plant your blueberries a little high to improve drainage. Mound soil around the base of the shrub to the crown of the plant, creating a gentle slope 2 to 3 inches high. The organic matter you added to the soil will help ensure quick drainage.

Plant blueberries in acidic, well-drained soil with the crown of the shrub 2 to 3 inches above soil level.

Quenching Their Thirst

Blueberries are shallow-rooted shrubs and need at least an inch of rain per week during the growing season. If they dry out, berries may fail to form, or fruit may shrivel on the bush. Organic matter improves moisture retention, and a thick mulch (4 to 5 inches) of acidic material (pine needles or composted leaves, for example) will help slow moisture loss. As this mulch decays over time, it keeps your soil nice and acidic.

Choosin' the Blues

Different types of blueberries are suited to different climates. Ask at your favorite nursery, or call the local Cooperative Extension office for recommendations.

Lowbush blueberries are very cold tolerant (Zone 2) and not well suited to warmer climates (south of Zone 7). Growing up in New Hampshire, I picked lowbush berries every summer in the White Mountains. When you're 10, you don't mind bending over for hours at a time, as long as the reward is fresh blueberry cobbler. Lowbush berries have the classic wild blueberry taste, about a million times better than those pumped-up, ridiculously bloated berries you find at the supermarket. Berries are small, so you'll have to pick a lot; encourage small children to help with this task.

Rabbit-eye blueberries are suited for warmer climates and are hardy to Zone 6 or 7, depending on the cultivar. They also tolerate slightly less acidic soils and are a little more drought tolerant than either lowbush or highbush varieties (see below). Most home gardeners prune rabbit-eye shrubs, because they can reach a height of 10 to 20 feet, which makes them difficult to pick and net (I'll get to netting in a minute).

Highbush blueberries thoughtfully put their berries conveniently within arms' reach. Shrubs grow to 6 to 8 feet tall. Cold hardiness varies with cultivars, but most require cold winters. Berries are numerous and sweet, and the shrubs are also nicely ornamental. If highbush blueberries suit your growing conditions, plant them.

Pick of the Crop

Most blueberries begin fruiting when they're 3 years old and most shrubs are sold as 2- or 3-year old plants, so you won't have to wait long for that first crop. Once you see berries start to form, wrap the shrub in netting to keep the birds off. You probably won't have to build a frame to hold the net away from the shrub; just wrap a piece of bird netting (available at garden centers and big box stores) around the shrub. Most birds freak out when their feet touch the net. To avoid getting tangled, they'll leave the bush alone.

Berries ripen over several weeks, so you'll probably pick a few times. Just because they're blue doesn't mean they're ready to harvest, however; sample before you haul out the basket. You should be able to get several pints of berries even from a small bush. Of course you'd be crazy not to eat as you pick . . . that's one of the joys of growing blueberries. But if you can't use them all right away, wash, dry, and freeze the berries until you have time to get creative.

Blueberries are nutritious and delicious. And versatile. You can make wine, jam, cake, ice cream — the list goes on and on. But remember, nobody doesn't like blueberries. So be *very* careful whom you invite over on a warm summer weekend in July.

Blueberry Smoothie

Makes 1 large glass

> 1 cup blueberries
> 1 banana
> 1 cup nonfat vanilla yogurt
> ½ cup skim milk
> ½ cup crushed ice

1. Purée all ingredients in a blender until smooth (it's a smoothie, right?) and sweeten to taste, if at all.

Blueberry Sauce

Makes 4 servings

> 2 cups blueberries
> ½ cup sugar
> 1 tablespoon lemon juice
> 1 cup water, divided
> 1 teaspoon cornstarch

1. Combine the blueberries, sugar, and lemon juice with ½ cup of the water in a saucepan and bring to a boil. Boil for 2 minutes, stirring constantly, then remove from heat. Taste and adjust by adding more lemon juice or sugar.

2. Dissolve the cornstarch in the remaining ½ cup of cold water, then add the solution to the hot berry sauce. Return to the heat and boil for 1 minute.

3. Pour the sauce over vanilla ice cream, angel food cake, or anything else your heart desires.

Stone
Accents for Your
Garden

Ancient Britons utilized astounding manpower to move stones weighing several tons apiece into standing circles perfectly positioned to mark the solar calendar. Thousands of buff, Bronze Age builders toiled for years to erect Stonehenge. You can have your own monument for considerably less time and trouble. Feel free to celebrate with the pagan ritual of your choice!

There's something tremendously satisfying about stone. Stone has personality. You want to touch it, you know you do. It can be cool, warm, smooth, craggy. It can communicate serenity or fiery upheaval. It comes in lots of colors. And it's free.

The shape of stone you choose depends on how you want to use it. A large flat stone can be laid at the front of a garden border with small succulents planted in the rock's natural hollows. A narrow standing stone is a vertical accent, dramatic against a backdrop of ornamental grasses. A small boulder with an appealing curve looks natural nestled into a clump of ferns.

What kind of rock do you have where you live? In my garden (which, as I've said, is in Rock City, PA), I have plenty of options. I keep a pile of spares behind the house. Every time I dig a hole, a new stone is added to the heap.

If your backyard isn't chock-full of rock, take a stroll in the neighborhood to see what you can find. Don't take anything without permission. That being said, it's pretty unusual for someone to complain about you walking away with a stray boulder. If you're shopping for a large stone, bring along some extra muscle. You won't necessarily need a phalanx of Druids, but a pair of helping hands couldn't hurt.

Piles of balanced stones (aka cairns) were used to mark sacred sites in ancient times.

Stepping stones can be interplanted with low-growing thymes.

A flat stone wall laid three or four rows high makes a neat edge for a low raised bed.

Flat Stones

If a flat boulder fits your garden aesthetic, look for one that offers something extra. Lichens come in many colors — orange, green, yellow, blue — and grow on rocks where the air is clean. A rock with a shallow hollow can be a planter for drought-tolerant plants. A flat stone can be a solar heater for cats or butterflies (but not both!) in the garden. Perhaps you'll find a lovely sedimentary rock with stripes of different colored minerals.

Stone Walls

Do you need a stone wall around a new garden bed? You can easily transform a collection of flat rocks into a natural border. Lay a single layer of stones around the edge of your garden. Begin the second layer by setting a stone over the space between the first two stones in the bottom row, then continue along. In this way the joints of each row are covered by the row above. A border three or four stones high makes an excellent garden wall.

Whether you opt for a vertical stone display or a horizontal one, you'll enjoy this low-maintenance garden monument for years to come. It provides an excellent accent during the growing season when its hard surfaces contrast with soft green foliage, and in the winter garden its color shows up beautifully against the snow. An ornament for all seasons.

Cue the fairy harps. The first rays of the rising sun appear above the horizon as the beat of the tabor sounds and wooden pan-pipes join in. Mist rises from the still waters of a dark lake, around a mysterious gray shape. The camera pulls back to reveal . . . your own personal Stonehenge. Now break out the mistletoe, pour some witches' brew, and get out there and sacrifice something.

For your own Stonehenge, find your ideal stone and haul it back to the garden, then move it into place to make sure you've found the perfect location. Look at each side, carefully evaluating the shapes and colors of the stone face. Later, after your stone is in place, think about planting something in front of it. This serves a dual purpose. Interesting foliage in front of a rock face accentuates the beauty of the stone and highlights the plant. It also makes the stone look as if it has been there for some time, in place naturally.

clear out and dig in

Dig a hole for your standing stone and move the rock into place. (P.S. Wear gloves. Rocks can be razor sharp. Think arrowheads and neolithic axes.) A good general rule is to bury the bottom third of a stone to make sure it's solid. Here's where that extra pair of hands comes in handy again.

set in stone

Ask your burly assistant to hold the stone in place while you step back and confirm the genius of your placement. Once you're satisfied, backfill the hole, tamping in the soil as you go. A 2×4 makes an excellent tool; use it to pound the soil tightly around the base of the standing stone.

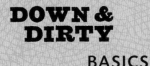

Knowing the Good Bugs from the Bad Bugs

31

I was afraid to garden as a child because the possibility of touching a worm freaked me out. Today I squish Japanese beetle larvae between my fingers to hear them pop, and never bat an eyelash. My, how times have changed!

Most humans have a negative, knee-jerk reaction to insects and their ilk. But so many bugs can be helpful in the garden, it pays to know which are friends and which are foes. Please allow me to introduce you to a handful of your garden neighbors. Some are arachnids, some are insects, there's even a mollusk in there. You're bound to meet a stranger every now and then, and if it's not stinging or biting you, I suggest doing a little research before you swat or squish. You can't exactly take it back once you've killed something.

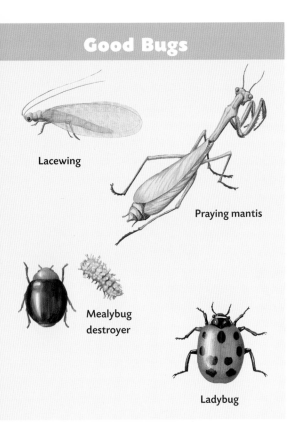

Good Bugs

Lacewing

Praying mantis

Mealybug
destroyer

Ladybug

The Good

Beneficial nematodes are small, unsegmented worms. Most nematodes are plant pests, microscopic parasites that damage roots. Beneficial nematodes are slightly larger (I still can't see them without a microscope), and they do several helpful things in the garden. They occur naturally in compost piles, where they help break down organic matter. They also feed on the larval stages of many destructive insects; if the pests live in the soil, chances are a beneficial nematode will find them tasty. But here's the cool part: Beneficial nematodes eat an insect from the inside out! They enter their prey through the mouth (or any other available opening) and hunker down for the long haul. They eat, they reproduce, and, yes, they excrete. It's actually a bacterium in nematode feces that kills the insect host. Which is more than you probably want to know, but I couldn't resist sharing.

You buy beneficial nematodes in a dormant stage and apply them to your lawn or garden in a water-based spray or through your irrigation system. Timing is crucial (usually evening, under moist conditions), so follow instructions from the supplier precisely.

Certain plants, such as this yarrow (*Achillea*) can attract "good" lacewings to your garden.

Lacewings are small green flying insects that are excellent general garden predators. Adults are ½ to ¾ inches long and bright green with transparent wings. They lay eggs on the tips of hairlike stalks on the undersides of leaves. Before I knew what they were, I wiped them off. My bad. The larval stage of this insect is voracious. They're nicknamed "aphid lions" because of the ferocious way they devour their favorite prey. They eat other insect pests including spider mites, soft scale, beetle larvae, and caterpillars. You can buy eggs or larvae commercially and place them throughout the garden. (The larvae are highly cannibalistic, and are packaged in mini–prison cells. You open the containers when you release the larvae in the garden.)

You can attract lacewings to your garden by planting flowers that produce plentiful pollen and nectar; these attractors include goldenrod, milkweed, Queen Ann's lace, sunflower, and yarrow.

Ladybugs are also known as convergent lady beetles. Both the adults and the larvae are voracious eaters. We all know what an adult lady beetle looks like (red or red-orange with black spots), but the red and black larvae are easily mistaken for something sinister. I don't know if it's because they're unfamiliar or because they're pointy with rough alligator skin. (If I didn't know what they were, my knees would certainly jerk.) Lady beetles are excellent aphid predators, and will eat other bad bugs as well. Release them as adults, but don't be alarmed if many of them immediately fly away. If you have a sufficient food source (that is, lots of tasty bugs), enough ladybugs will stick around to do the job. They're a great choice for getting started with beneficial insects, and a friendly folkloric symbol. No one's afraid of a ladybug. Chances are you'll find them in your garden naturally.

Mealybug destroyers. Doesn't this sound like the Godzilla of insect predators? I love the image of a giant mealybug destroyer lumbering through the garden looking for mealybugs. Another common name for this beneficial insect is crypt (short for *Cryptolaemus*). This is a type of ladybug beetle. The adults are black with a reddish head. Both larvae and adults eat mealybug eggs and mealybugs, and when those are gone, they'll eat whatever other insects they can get their jaws into. Crypts are shipped as adult females,

The Scoop on IPM

The National IPM network defines Integrated Pest Management: IPM is a sustainable approach to managing pests by combining biological, cultural, physical, and chemical tools in a way that minimizes economic, health, and environmental risks.

IPM is a multipronged pest-management strategy that focuses on long-term prevention. You don't just whip out a can of Raid. You begin with healthy, well-sited plants that are strong and resistant to predation. Observe your plants carefully and regularly, so you notice a problem before it grows to epidemic proportions. Correctly ID the specific pest that plagues you and learn a little about its lifecycle so you can act when it's most vulnerable. Remove the pest physically, either manually or using good bugs! And as a last resort, you can use chemicals, but always start with the least toxic method that will also be effective.

Where's the Closest Bug Store?

Obviously, you can't go down to the corner store and pick up a bag of lacewings. As beneficial insects become more popular, however, they are also more readily available. Nurseries committed to the principles of Integrated Pest Management will often carry or order beneficial insects for their customers. There are also mail-order companies that carry a wide range of beneficials. My favorite is The Green Spot, which is based in New Hampshire. These guys really know their stuff and are very generous with their time, helping you figure out which beneficial insects are right for your growing situation. For Web site information, see Resources in the appendix.

which lay their eggs in the cottony white egg masses of mealybugs. In their larval stage, crypts look a lot like their prey, but they grow considerably larger (up to 1 cm). Mealybug destroyers do their thing indoors too, so they're effective for your houseplants as well as outdoors.

Praying mantids. I don't recommend using the praying mantis as a beneficial insect, but I know most people expect to find it listed that way. Let me take this opportunity, then, to set you straight. Praying mantids (weird plural form) eat without discrimination, meaning they devour good bugs as well as bad bugs. They'll eat butterflies and moths, and have even been known to kill the smallest species of hummingbirds. They'll also eat each other, given half a chance. So I can't recommend them for use against specific insect pests. *But,* if you're trying to get your kids interested in nature, these insects are dramatic enough to fascinate any child. Watching 100 mantids hatch out of an egg case (and then seeing the fast ones feed on the slower ones) is pretty cool if you're a 10-year-old. Hell, it's interesting if you're 35. Still, don't expect them to solve your garden-pest problems, and never put them in the butterfly or hummingbird garden!

The Bad

These are the annoying bugs, the bugs that disfigure but don't necessarily kill. Still, we don't want them around. We've worked hard to make the garden grow, so why hand it over to the ravenous hordes?

Lace bugs. Different types of lace bugs (not to be confused with lacewings) feed on a variety of garden plants, including andromeda, juneberry, hawthorn, and cotoneaster. Larvae and adults feed on the undersides of leaves until only dead tissue remains. Lace bugs don't necessarily kill a tree or shrub, but they cause aesthetic damage and leaves may drop prematurely, which weakens the plant. Prune away damaged parts and spray with a light horticultural oil. Lace bugs are drawn to stressed plants, so site your plants correctly and monitor recently transplanted or stressed specimens. For natural predators, try ladybugs and lacewings.

Leaf miners. These are the larval form of a small fly that lays its eggs on the undersides of leaves. The eggs hatch and larvae penetrate the leaf tissue, then feed inside the leaf, leaving white tunnels of empty space behind them. The trails are unmistakable. Once, at a salad bar, I noticed that the spinach had leaf miners. Needless to say, the prospect of eating larvae and their feces did not appeal to me, so I passed on the spinach.

Leaf miners are easy to control if you notice them soon enough. Remove any damaged leaves from a plant and throw them away. (Don't compost them.) At the end of the season, be sure to pick up any plant debris in the area where you spotted leaf miners.

Scale and mealybugs. Scale and mealybugs move slowly, so if you catch them quickly, you can get rid of them with a horticultural oil or beneficial insects. But they don't look like your typical insect pests, so it's easy to let them go until they've reached epidemic proportions. Scale look like brown bumps on bark or leaves. Adults don't move, but you can scrape them off with a fingernail. This is a good test: If it scrapes off, it's scale. If it doesn't, it's bark. Mealybugs are a soft scale and are covered with a white, cottony coating. Both suck the life juices out of plant tissue (indoors and out) and can do substantial damage if left unchecked. So check.

Slugs. A slug is a snail without a shell; in other words, it's a mollusk. You usually don't see the slug itself — you see the silvery trail (solidified mucus!) left behind on plant leaves and you see holes in those leaves. Adult slugs spend the day in the cool shade, under rocks or pots; they come out at night to feed. Place a few saucers of beer among their favorite plants; this lures them in and dissolves them. There are also effective commercial products on the market, but be sure to read labels carefully. Some aren't safe to use around pets and wild birds, and may contaminate groundwater. If you're really hard core, you can always pick them off plants with your fingers and crush them underfoot.

Spittle bugs. Usually people notice the spittle rather than the bugs. The foamy mass protects a young stage of the insect (a nymph); if you see it, wipe it off and smush it between your fingers. (You'll probably want to wear

These silvery trails are a classic indication of leaf miner predation.

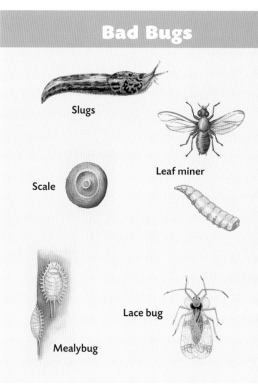

Bad Bugs

Slugs

Leaf miner

Scale

Lace bug

Mealybug

gloves.) Both adults and nymphs are sucking insects that love strawberries but feed on other plants as well. The damage is rarely dreadful, but plants can be stunted and weakened, which reduces yield. It's best to get rid of the insects as you go along. If you've had a lot of spittle bugs, cut back and dispose of the susceptible plants where eggs might overwinter.

The Very Bad

The jury is in and the sentence is death.

Aphids. Aphids bear live young *and* lay eggs. They have *so* got the reproductive thing covered. It's not difficult to get rid of aphids as long as you catch them soon enough. They reproduce so quickly that there are often aphids of numerous sizes clustered, pulsating, heaving like a single mass as they feed on the lifeblood of our beloved plants. If you spot them early, a strong blast of water from the hose may be all you need to get rid of them, or use insecticidal soap. Left untreated, aphids can quickly defoliate both perennial and annual plants. They come in green, black, orange, or white.

Gypsy moth caterpillars. Bad bad bad bad bad bad bad. These caterpillars will quickly defoliate a mature oak, making it look like April in July. Oaks are a preferred food, but gypsy moth caterpillars eat a wide range of tree foliage, including conifers. Deciduous trees can tolerate 1 year's defoliation but 2 or 3 years in a row may fell even a mighty oak. A hard-hit conifer can die in a single season. Females lay masses of eggs under a light tan protective covering in late summer. Eggs hatch in May and caterpillars eat throughout the summer. Scrape off as many egg cases as you can and burn the eggs or dump them in soapy water. Kill every caterpillar you can get your hands on. And if you have to call in the big guns, then pick up the phone.

Japanese beetles. Adults skeletonize the foliage of many kinds of plants, sometimes defoliating them entirely. They also devour flowers. The larvae are disgusting, plump white grubs that live in the soil and munch on the roots of your lawn. Skunks love to eat them, and will dig up patches of grass in search of the grubs. If you encounter the grubs while digging, squeeze them between your fingers. They make a superbly satisfying pop. Pick off

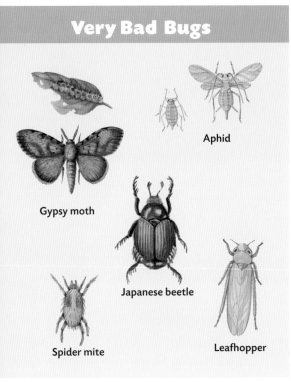

Very Bad Bugs

Aphid

Gypsy moth

Japanese beetle

Spider mite

Leafhopper

adults from plants by hand and crush them or toss them in a bucket of soapy water. Or spray beneficial nematodes on nearby soil. Do this at the first sign of a problem. *Do not* use pheromone traps for the adults. Many people think these do more harm than good, bringing more Japanese beetles to your garden than they actually kill.

Leafhoppers. These little buggers move fast, so you have to be quick to catch them. Adults are green or brown and some have bright red markings. Both adults and nymphs feed on leaves and flowers, and their saliva is toxic to plants. The toxins stunt growth; leaves turn yellow and become distorted. Leafhoppers can also spread viral diseases as they feed. Spray with insecticidal soap (if you can catch them), but if the insects are on edible plants, don't use any toxic chemicals. Parasitic wasps are an effective predator against leafhoppers.

Spider mites. These arachnids (they have eight legs) are tough pests to conquer. In hot weather they multiply very rapidly, and since they're so tiny, it's difficult to spot them until the population is overwhelming. They are also resistant to many pesticides and require intense chemicals to kill them. Your best bet is to monitor plants carefully. As soon as you see the first sign of spider mites (silvery stippling on leaves, webbing in leaf axils — the angle between the stem of the plant and the leaf stem), prune off damaged plant parts and spray with an insecticidal soap. Predatory mites eat spider mites and can be used to control them outdoors. They're available from most reputable bug stores.

It's a big wide world out there, and there are lots of bugs in it. Get to know which ones to work with, which ones to live with, and which ones to terminate with extreme prejudice.

Safe Sprays

Sometimes you can control a pest simply by removing it from the plant. Other times you have to spray. Soap and water make a nontoxic spray that's effective against aphids and a few other pests. Use a generous squirt of dishwashing liquid to a pint of water and apply with a spray mister. Horticultural oils are reasonably safe, oil-based sprays that are lightweight enough to use year-round. (Dormant oil sprays are heavier and can be used only when a plant is dormant.) The label of each horticultural oil will tell you how close to harvest you can use the spray on edible plants.

A Cutting Garden for All Seasons

What exactly is a cutting garden? In my book (literally) it's any garden you grow with the intention of cutting plants for display. Did you notice I didn't say anything about pretty flowers? Sure, a cutting garden may include pretty flowers, but why limit yourself? Evergreen boughs, interesting branches, cuttings from shrubs and bulbs, all these things can be part of a cutting garden for all seasons.

What do you want from a cutting garden? Flowers in summer? Boughs and berries in fall? Cut arrangements all year long? Now we're talkin'. Here are 15 garden plants you can cut and enjoy from winter through fall. And we're not even scratching the surface.

Forsythia (*Forsythia* species and hybrids)

Tulips (*Tulipa* species and hybrids)

Peonies (*Paeonia* species and hybrids)

Love-in-a-Mist *(Nigella damascena)*

Year-Round Cutting-Garden Plants

Forsythia (*Forsythia* species and hybrids)

The branches of this shrub may look bare in the winter garden, but indoors, they'll put on a bold yellow show. Cut forsythia January through March and place the branches in warm water to encourage flower buds to open. Zone 5.

Tulips (*Tulipa* species and hybrids)

Cut tulip flowers when the buds are flushed with color but not yet open. What better way to bring spring inside the house than with a vase of long-stemmed hybrid tulips or a bowl of small species tulips? Zones 3–8, depending on type.

Peonies (*Paeonia* species and hybrids)

Traditionally, cutting garden flowers are called "cut-and-come-again." You cut the flowers for your arrangement and the plant obligingly produces another round. Peonies are a different story. These perennials put on a great show only once a year, but boy, what a show it is. Peonies are extravagantly luscious, from tight bud to blowsy, flung-open, spent flower. Cut a couple for an indulgent display. Zone 3.

Love-in-a-Mist *(Nigella damascena)*

You get both beautiful flowers and interesting seedpods from this annual. Shades of blues and purples give you a variety of color from one plant. These flowers also dry well for everlasting arrangements. Annual.

Zinnias (*Zinnia* hybrids)

These are classic garden annuals; treat them right and they'll bloom until frost. Zinnias come in many sizes and lots of bright, sunny colors. They'll put out new flowers as long you conscientiously deadhead them. Cutting blooms for indoor display guarantees a constant crop. Annual.

Zinnias (*Zinnia* hybrids)

Globe Thistle *(Echinops ritro)*

Not only is this an excellent, drought-tolerant perennial plant, but the round, blue flower adds structure to a bouquet as well. Its unusual shape and color work well in combination with other summer blooms, or try a big bunch of globe thistle for a contemporary display. Zone 3.

Globe Thistle *(Echinops ritro)*

Cosmos *(Cosmos bipinnatus)*

Even in the dog days of summer, there's something cool and classic about cosmos. Perhaps it's the lacy foliage or the pale pink and white flowers. (But then there are the magentas . . .) It's easy to grow from seed and puts out flowers all summer long; feel free to cut and cut and cut. Annual.

Cosmos *(Cosmos bipinnatus)*

Yarrow *(Achillea millefolium)*

This perennial usually produces another round of bloom after cutting. Foliage is feathery, and flowers come in white, yellows, pinks, reds, terra-cotta, and combinations. This plant is also drought tolerant. Zone 3.

Yarrow *(Achillea millefolium)*

Queen Anne's Lace *(Daucus carota)*

Queen Anne's Lace *(Daucus carota)*

If someone dismisses this plant as a mere roadside weed, he or she clearly has no soul. Queen Anne's lace *is* a roadside weed, of course, but it's also a beautiful cut flower and attracts good pollinators to your garden. This biennial is very drought tolerant. Zone 3.

Hydrangeas *(Hydrangea* species and hybrids)

Hydrangeas (*Hydrangea* species and hybrids)

These are excellent shrubs for a cutting garden. The flowers make showy fresh bouquets *and* lovely dried arrangements. The snowball and peegee varieties are better candidates for drying than is the lacecap, but fresh lacecap flowers are divine. Various zones.

Lion's Tail *(Leonotis leonurus)*

Lion's Tail *(Leonotis leonurus)*

Bright orange flowers make this a natural focal point. Stems are tall with blooms stacked one on top of the other. It's an unusual-looking flower, in its glory from late summer until frost. Annual.

Joe-Pye Weed *(Eupatorium purpureum)*

Joe-Pye Weed *(Eupatorium purpureum)*

I don't know why more people don't grow Joe-Pye weed. It may be too large for some gardens (6 to 8 feet tall), although a few cultivars are 4 to 4½ feet tall. It's a gorgeous perennial, with huge flat clusters of numerous dusky purple-pink flowers. The flower head can be 8 to 12 inches across and makes an excellent cut bloom. Zone 4.

Firethorn *(Pyracantha coccinea)*

Watch out for thorns; they're fierce! That being said, this is a voluptuous shrub, crowded with berries in shades of orange, vermilion, and red, depending on cultivar. Branches are superb in fall arrangements. Plus you can make jelly out of the berries. *Mmmmm.* Jelly. Zone 5.

Winterberry *(Ilex verticillata)*

This deciduous holly shows off its berries in fall and winter. Cut branches last for months. Hollies have separate male and female plants, and only females produce the bright berries. You'll need to have at least one male shrub in the vicinity to guarantee that your females produce their showy crop. Zone 4.

Red- or Yellow-Twig Dogwood (*Cornus alba* cultivars)

Not only is this an excellent shrub for the shade garden, but its variegated leaves are also useful in cut arrangements during the growing season. In winter, when the leaves have fallen, the bright red or yellow bark of the bare twigs is outstanding. Cut stems provide excellent color and structure for an arrangement. Zone 3.

There. I've thrown down the gauntlet. Move beyond the traditional bouquet by using evergreen branches, ornamental grass plumes, or sculptural magnolia seedheads in your arrangements. If you like the way it looks, try it in a vase. What's the worst that can happen? If you hate it, there are always the pretty flowers.

Firethorn *(Pyracantha coccinea)*

Winterberry *(Ilex verticillata)*

Red- and Yellow-Twig Dogwood (*Cornus alba* cultivars)

Tropical Plants for a Temperate Clime

33

If you live in Hawaii, go ahead and skip this chapter. South Florida? Skip it. But for all us poor saps who live where it freezes, well, this one's for us.

I don't understand why anyone is intimidated by the mere mention of tropical plants. It's not like they're any more difficult to grow than other plants. They just can't tolerate temperatures below freezing. If you stop and think about it, then this means that in principle you could grow tropicals in your garden during the time of year when temperatures are above freezing. Hmmm, doesn't that sound like how we grow . . . annuals?

Many tropicals, such as this ornamental ginger, have large showy leaves, sometimes with interesting varigations.

Ben divides an ornamental ginger.

A lot of our favorite garden annuals are tropical plants. In their native habitats, these plants aren't true annuals, of course. (The definition of an annual is a plant that completes its life cycle in 1 year. In other words, you plant the seed, the plant grows, it flowers, it produces seeds, and it dies.) In temperate climates, however, tropicals die when the temperature dips below freezing, so we call them annuals because we only get one year out of them. My point is, if you've ever grown a coleus (or a begonia or a browallia), you've grown a tropical plant. It wasn't difficult; you didn't even know you were doing anything special.

In the spirit of full disclosure I must tell you that I adore tropical plants. My house is full of them and I see no reason why they shouldn't be used outdoors as well. We've all felt the lure of sunny islands, fantasized about wandering through a tropical paradise while the sweet scents of jasmine and gardenia waft past on a gentle breeze. Don't have the airfare? Start digging.

Tropicals can be huge and showy. In a single season outdoors they grow *much* larger than they'll ever get indoors. This is because, in pots, root space is limited and root mass is proportional to shoot mass. If the roots can spread indefinitely, the aboveground portion of the plant will also grow like crazy. Plus, outdoor growing conditions in summer are often remarkably close to those of the tropics: long days of natural sunlight, soft rains, good air circulation, perhaps elevated humidity, depending on your location. Tropical plants won't even know they're outside their native clime.

Not all tropicals require high humidity and full sun. The tropical landscape is hugely varied and encompasses deserts, cloud forests, open plains, and shady jungles. Which means that wherever you are — Santa Fe, Bangor, or the Bronx — you can find a group of tropicals that will work for you.

Keeping Them Going

At the end of the summer, *before* a killing frost, take a look at your tropicals and see if there are any you've fallen in love with over the course of the summer. It can happen. The love between a gardener and his or her plants is a sacred thing.

If you're smitten, you can overwinter tropicals in several ways, depending on the plants and your indoor growing space. For example: If you've grown caladiums, overwinter them as dormant tubers in a cool, dark closet or basement (see Winterize!, page 222). If you've grown flowering maples, cut them back to about 6 inches tall, pot them up, and move them to a sunny windowsill until next spring.

Frankly, you're not obligated to overwinter any tropicals at all. Let 'em all die in the frost, cut them back, and start over again next year, maybe with a different color palette of plants. Their quick growth means even a new garden can look large and established after just a month or two.

Tropicals are so flamboyant and extravagant. Nothing says "Notice me!" like a 6-foot castor bean plant with fuzzy red seeds. So, if your tastes run to the wild, try a tropical garden. If you don't like it, no harm done. The plants will die soon and you can put something else there next year. But how much do you want to bet you get hooked?

Elephant ears (*Caladium* hybrid) are perfect for shade.

This young tropical garden will double or triple in size by the end of summer.

181

Planting a garden of tropical plants isn't much different from planting any other garden. You evaluate the available light the same way, prep the soil the same way, place the plants the same way, take the plants out of their pots the same way, plant them the same way, water the same way. And if you're growing in containers, well, still do it all the same way! Having said that, there are a few differences:

❀ Tropical plants will probably grow more quickly than your average perennial. For example, variegated cassava (*Manihot esculenta* 'Variegata') will go from 6 inches to 6 feet in just a few months. Plan accordingly.

❀ Many tropicals are heavy feeders, so fertilize them more often than you do your perennials. My general rule is to feed once every 2 weeks when daytime temps are in the 70s, once a month when they're in the 60s, not at all in the 50s.

the kindest cut

You may have to use a knife or scissors to cut the side of the pot to free your plant. If the plant's stuck in a clay pot, give the pot a whack with your trowel to break it.

two for one

If the plant is large, like this variegated ginger, use a pruning saw to cut it into two (or more) pieces.

treat 'em to good soil

Dig a planting hole just deep enough so that the plant will sit at the height it was growing in the pot and about one and a half times wider than the pot. Before you set the plant in place, mix some compost into the soil you removed.

give 'em a firm hand

Place the plant, then pour the soil around the plant and press it firmly into place; water thoroughly.

it's for the birds

It's mandatory to decorate a tropical garden with some kind of tropical-garden art. I like my brightly colored birds with spring-mounted wings that move in the breeze. But if your taste runs more toward stationary pink flamingos, by all means . . .

Tempting Tropicals

	Common name	Botanical Name	Moisture Requirements	Mature Height (in 1 Season)	Bonus Features
TROPICALS FOR A SUNNY SPOT	Angel's trumpets	*Brugmansia* hybrids	Well-drained soil	3–6'	Crazy big fragrant flowers; deer resistant
	Cassava	*Manihot esculenta*	Moist soil	4–6'	Large, deeply lobed leaves; very fast grower
	Castor bean	*Ricinus communis* 'Carmencita'	Well-drained soil	5–8'	Fuzzy red seeds; huge reddish leaves
	Chenille plant	*Acalypha hispida*	Moist soil	2–3'	Long (4–8"), velvety red flower tassels
	Horsetail	*Chondropetalum techtorum*	Moist soil	12–18"	Slim, leafless stems; very sleek and primitive
	Ornamental banana	*Musa acuminata, Ensete ventricosum*	Moist soil	3–6'	Large leaves with splashes of red (no fruit); both take some shade
	Persian shield	*Strobilanthes dyerianus*	Well-drained soil	2–5'	Purple and silver leaves
	Plumbago	*Plumbago auriculata*	Drought tolerant	2–6'	Numerous clumps of sky-blue flowers
	Snake plants	*Sansevieria* species and hybrids	Drought tolerant	1–4'	Large, stiff, succulent foliage
	Solanum	*Solanum pyracanthum*	Well-drained soil	1–2'	Purple flowers, orange thorns

	Common Name	Botanical Name	Moisture Requirements	Mature Height (in 1 Season)	Bonus Features
TROPICALS FOR A SHADY SPOT	Begonias	*Begonia* species and hybrids	Well-drained soil	1–5'	Many varieties; wild foliage variegation; flowers
	Coleus	*Solanostemon scutellariodes*	Well-drained soil	1–2'	Most excellent foliage
	Elephant's ears	*Caladium* hybrids	Moist soil	1–2'	Crazy variegation on large leaves
	Flowering maples	*Abutilon* hybrids	Well-drained soil	1–3'	Bell-shaped flowers; variegated foliage
	Lady palm	*Rhapis excelsa*	Well-drained soil	2–5'	Large compound leaves; classic tropical feel
	Mosaic plant	*Fittonia verschaffeltii*	Moist soil	6–8'	Heavily veined leaves, pink or white on green
	Ornamental ginger	*Alpinia zerumbet* 'Variegata'	Moist soil	3–4'	Yellow-and-green-striped leaves
	Peacock moss	*Selaginella uncinata*	Moist soil	2–3"	Ground cover; feathery, blue-green leaves
	Ribbon bush	*Homalocladium platycladum*	Well-drained soil	2–4'	Flat, leafless, segmented stems; unique growth habit
	Ti plant	*Cordyline terminalis*	Moist soil	3–4'	Large, variegated leaves

Multiply
Your Plants by
Dividing

34

It is, in fact, possible to have too much of a good thing. Well, too much of a good thing in one place, that is. If your garden is thriving, you've probably noticed that your perennials get bigger each year. Eventually, they become crowded and you need to give them room to breathe.

Some plants require division every few years to maintain vigor. For example, yarrow, daylilies, and hardy geraniums may become thin at the center of the clump, producing fewer, smaller flowers and generally looking weak. Division will rejuvenate a plant.

Divide dayilies every three years to keep them vigorous.

If you want to win friends and influence people, consider dividing plants to offer as bribes. I mean gifts. Who doesn't like a free plant every now and then? Collect 'em, grow 'em, trade 'em with your friends. Gardeners are always offering plants to each other. It's what we do.

But exactly *when* do we do it? The timing depends on when a plant blooms. Divide spring-flowering plants in fall; summer- and fall-flowering plants may be divided either in spring or after they finish blooming in fall. Dividing just before bloom time won't kill plants, but it may prevent them from flowering that year.

If you have a choice, I say do it in the fall. That way, when plants come up the following spring, they resume their natural, rounded shape. A perennial that's been cut in half in spring will keep its oddly semicircular shape all season long.

An Exception for Everything: Bearded Iris

Everyone should grow bearded iris. They're low maintenance, drought tolerant, and deer resistant, and they have complex flowers in a huge range of colors, as well as foliage that's attractive enough to grow for its own sake. Iris spread via rhizomes along the top of the soil, sending out roots from the bottom and leaves from the top. Divide these immediately after flowering stops, which is usually in late July or August. Dig up the rhizomes and squeeze them. If a piece feels mushy, get rid of it. Break the rhizomes by hand at the obvious joints or use pruners if you prefer. Replant the rhizomes, leaving the tops visible at soil level, and water well. To reduce stress, cut back the foliage to about 6 inches. New growth should resume within 4 to 6 weeks and you'll have flowers again next year.

Plant Tip: Rhizomes are modified plant stems that grow horizontally underground, or just along the soil surface. They grow from the base of a plant and spread outward, enabling the plant to grow larger as the rhizome spreads. Roots grow down from the bottom of the rhizome; stems and leaves grow up from the top. The fresh ginger you buy at a grocery store is an edible rhizome. Lay it flat on top of some potting soil (in a pot!) and bury it about halfway, leaving the top of the rhizome visible. Water once, then wait for it to sprout. Presto! Instant houseplant.

Be Prepared

Before you do the deed, prepare. Water the plant that's going to be divided a day in advance. This makes the soil easier to work with. Think about where the divided perennials are going to go and have the holes or pots ready for them. The less time these plants spend with their roots exposed to the drying air, the less trauma they'll experience. Also, don't perform the surgery at the hottest time of day, with the sun directly overhead. Heat dries out the plant and increases stress.

Perennials that produce distinct crowns or spread by underground stems are well-suited to division. Some, such as bee balm (*Monarda didyma*, Zone 3) and barrenworts (*Epimedium* species, Zone 5), can be divided with your bare hands, almost. Dig up a plant (with a shovel, hence the "almost") and lay it out on the ground. You'll be able to tug apart individual plants without any additional gear.

After you've replanted your divided plants in their new location, the new transplants may need extra TLC for a few weeks, while their roots get established. A good general rule is to allow plants 6 weeks of nonstressful recuperation after a traumatic division and transplant. This means don't do it in the heat of summer or right before a frost. A plant should have 6 weeks of moderate temperatures to recover from surgery.

It's a little scary the first time you divide a plant, but it's an important step for any beginning gardener. Like riding a bike without training wheels. Once you see how easy it is, your chest will swell with pride as you casually mention, "Yeah, I divided my daylilies this morning. I have some extra. Do you want any?"

Bee balm (*Monarda didyma*) (above) and barrenwort (*Epimedium* species) (below) are two vigorous growers that are easy to divide.

Hostas have thick, fleshy roots that form a solid clump. To make dividing a muscular root system easier, you'll need a few tools. Use a transplanting shovel (see Cool Tools, pages 39–43) to dig up the plant. Be careful not to snap the handle of your spade or to fall and hurt yourself. I have done both and there is no dignity in either. You may have to get down on your hands and knees to cut a few stubborn roots and release the root-ball. Don't let fear make you tentative; the hosta can handle it. If you must, whistle a happy tune.

When you have the hosta out of the ground, place it on its side on a tarp and examine it at soil level. How many individual crowns does it have? How many smaller plants would you like to create? How large would you like those plants to be? Here's how to proceed.

pry 'em out

Dig a perimeter into the soil 3 to 4 inches beyond the base of the plant to be divided. To loosen the root-ball, dig down and toward the center. You may need to pry with the shovel, using a gentle rocking motion until you can lift the plant out. Lay the plant on a tarp.

the kindest cut

Choose the place for the first cut, making sure it's between two crowns. With the plant still on its side, place the tines of one garden fork on the root-ball at the point where you'd like to divide. With a firm, swift push, stab the tines through the roots and soil. Assuming your tarp isn't made of gold brocade, it's no big deal if the tines poke a few holes in it.

pull 'em apart

Line up a second garden fork with the first one, back to back, so the tines are between those of the first fork. Push the second fork into the root-ball with a strong, swift motion. With one hand on each garden fork, gently push them away from each other, outward toward the edges of the plant. The root-ball should pull apart easily, along the line established by the two forks. You may need to rock the forks back and forth a little, or do some final detangling by hand. Repeat this sequence as many times as you must to get the number and size of divisions you want.

back in the ground

Take the new plants and replant them as soon as possible. Be sure to replant at the original depth, leaving the plant enough room to grow for another 3 years. Firm the soil around the roots and water well.

35

An Evening Garden that Glows in the Dark

People work hard. They work long hours and they don't get home till late. Sometimes it's already dark. So how are we hardworking people supposed to enjoy our gardens? We can plant a garden that glows in the dark. I'm not talking about Day-Glo paint or black-light posters. White flowers and silver foliage really pop in the evening, creating a subtle shimmer in the garden.

Let's indulge several senses while we're at it. Some flowers are especially fragrant after dark. They're pollinated by night-flying creatures (moths and bats, for example); once the sun goes down, night-bloomers

Bats!

Please don't wig out about bats. Bats are cool, helpful, and good for you and your garden, yet people often get all freaky when I suggest putting up a bat house or wax poetic about all the good bats do. First of all, if you already have bats in your garden, be glad. Bats are winged exterminators, flying through the air with their mouths open, scooping up mosquitoes, blackflies, and other insects as if they were candy. Which they are. To a bat. And second, it takes more than a few night-blooming plants to attract bats. I've had a bat house in my yard for years but remain alone and disappointed. Apparently I can't offer them just the right combination of warm shelter and a nearby water source, although the lake is only 1,000 feet away, as the bat flies. If you have bats, consider yourself lucky. They don't bite, they don't get tangled in your hair, and you're more likely to get rabies from the raccoon that gets into your garbage.

pull out all the stops, looking good and smelling fine. Plant a selection of these for a garden that's at its best during the cocktail hour, when even the hardest-working multitasker is kicking back with her feet up on the railing.

Light colors stand out best in the dark, so select flowers of white, pale pink, silver, and pale yellow. Silver foliage and leaves with white variegation also make a strong visual statement. A combination of these, with some darker-leaved plants to provide a backdrop, will give you a landscape to admire even after the sun has set.

White flowers and foliage are useful in every garden, of course, but in an evening garden they are downright necessary. If you frequently find yourself sitting on the deck in the gloaming, consider giving yourself something special to look at. Then pour yourself a glass of whatever, sit back, and smell the moonflowers.

My Favorite Glow-in-the-Dark Plants

Angel's Trumpets (*Brugmansia* species and hybrids)

Tropical plants that do best in full sun, angel's trumpets can grow to 4 to 6 feet tall in a single season. Treat them as annuals in climates where temperatures go below freezing. Large (6 to 8 inches), pendent flowers come in many pale colors that show up well in the dark. Most are highly fragrant. Annual.

Angel's Trumpets (*Brugmansia* species and hybrids)

Caladiums (*Caladium* hybrids)

Caladiums are great plants for a regular daytime shady garden, but in an evening garden they rock. Intricate patterns on the large leaves create a backdrop of subtle shades and silver reflections that undulate in the slightest breeze. Caladiums grow best in shade and moist soil. Plant them with white impatiens for a combination of flower and foliage that shines at dusk. Annual.

Diamond Frost (*Euphorbia* 'Diamond Frost')

This outstanding plant grows in full to part sun, in containers, or in the ground. Dainty, oval, blue-green leaves punctuate slim round stems. Small white flowers are held above the leaves, sprinkled liberally over the entire plant. The effect is foamy and delicate. Diamond Frost is drought tolerant. It has a sprawling habit, so use it at the front of a display, where it can tumble. Annual.

Dusty Miller (*Centaurea cineraria* 'Colchester White')

Although dusty miller isn't the most unusual plant, it's peerless in the evening garden. There are several plants with the common name dusty miller and all have bright silvery foliage. 'Colchester White' is my favorite because its leaves are very finely cut, like the teeth of a feathery comb. Dusty miller is drought tolerant and grows best in sun, but it will take some shade. This is a tender perennial and may be hardy in your area depending on the cultivar. Pinch off the flowers to concentrate the plant's resources on foliage rather than bloom. Zone 8.

Caladiums (*Caladium* hybrids)

Diamond Frost (*Euphorbia* 'Diamond Frost')

Dusty Miller (*Centaurea cineraria* 'Colchester White')

Flowering Tobacco *(Nicotiana sylvestris)*

Goatsbeard *(Aruncus dioicus)*

Montauk Daisy *(Nipponanthemum nipponicum)*

Flowering Tobacco *(Nicotiana sylvestris)*

Flowering tobacco is an excellent annual that fills many specialty niches: It flowers well in shade, it self-seeds *very* reliably, and it's deer resistant. A basal rosette of large, hairy, yellow-green leaves is topped by a bloom stalk 3 to 6 feet tall. Small, white, tubular flowers are very fragrant. *N. langsdorffii* is similar but has pale green flowers, also fragrant. Annual.

Goatsbeard *(Aruncus dioicus)*

An excellent tall perennial for a shady garden, goatsbeard grows to 4 to 6 feet tall. Finely cut foliage is topped by branching plumes of tiny cream-colored flowers. The bloom itself is about a foot tall, and very delicate. Goatsbeard flowers in late spring and will often self-seed if you don't deadhead immediately. Leave the dried flowers for 3 to 4 weeks if you'd like seedlings next year. Zone 4.

Montauk Daisy *(Nipponanthemum nipponicum)*

Blooming at the same time as chrysanthemums, Montauk daisy should be pinched back in a similar manner. To avoid tall, floppy, early-blooming plants, cut back all the stems to about 4 inches at the beginning of June, then again in late July. You'll be rewarded in September and October with large (3- to 4-inch diameter), daisylike flowers that gleam in the twilight. Montauk daisy grows best in full sun. Zone 5.

Moonflower *(Ipomoea alba)*

This vining annual produces large white flowers, 4 to 6 inches in diameter. Sow seeds directly in the ground; they don't respond well to transplanting. Moonflower starts slowly but finishes with a big bang, hitting its stride in late August through September. Flowers open as the sun sets and may stay open on cloudy days; they are richly fragrant. Don't overfertilize or you'll get lots of leaves and few flowers. Annual.

Silver Falls *(Dichondra argentea)*

The trailing leaves and stems of Silver Falls are perfect for a hanging basket or as a ground cover. It fills in quickly at the base of trees and shrubs, creating a cushion of soft, silvery white. Leaves are small and shiny, with an unusual fan shape. In a basket, stems cascade over the edges as much as 3 to 5 feet. This plant is drought tolerant and grows best in full to part sun. Annual.

Sweet Autumn Clematis (*Clematis terniflora,* formerly *C. paniculata*)

Sweet autumn clematis flowers in September and October, depending on your zone. It's a magical vine, transforming from plain green leaves meandering up a trellis to an explosion of dainty white blooms, a haze, a cloud, a blanket of white. Very fragrant, very showy. As with all clematis, grow it in full sun, but give the roots some shade, either by planting a ground cover, using a heavy mulch, or setting a few flat rocks at the base of the plant. Zone 5.

Moonflower *(Ipomoea alba)*

Silver Falls *(Dichondra argentea)*

Sweet Autumn Clematis (*Clematis terniflora,* formerly *C. paniculata*)

Safe and Easy Wild Foods

36

My sister Elizabeth says that come the apocalypse, she's heading for my house. I'm not sure how she'll get here with the roads all clogged with the twisted carcasses of metal vehicles and heavy machinery, but she's welcome to try. Because not only do I have a well-stocked pantry of preserved foods, but I also know a thing or two about wild edibles. In other words, if you get lost in the woods, you want me with you (and not just because I can read a map).

My nephews stare at me with disbelief when I pull a berry off a tree and pop it into my mouth. What do I expect? They live in Boston. The truth is, you can forage almost anywhere, even in the middle of the biggest city. And I love introducing kids to the wonders of the harvest. It's simple to start with a few foolproof wild foods. Go for a walk and enjoy the bounty you find along the way. Here are five wild foods you'll be able to find and enjoy almost anywhere:

Cattail pollen. You may not think of cattails as having flowers, but that's what the brown, brushlike thing at the top of the plant is. When the male flowers are in full bloom, they're covered with a thick coat of mustard yellow pollen. Depending on where you live, it's ready for harvest in mid- to late July. Watch for it! Cover the flower head with a paper bag and shake it to collect the pollen, which makes a unique, lightweight flour. Try substituting it for half the flour in a pancake recipe to make extra-fluffy flapjacks.

Dandelion. This is the classic early-spring green. Pick it before it flowers; later, foliage is bitter and tough. Dandelion leaves make an excellent raw salad green, or steam them and serve with lemon juice and a little olive oil. They have lots of vitamins A and C, plus iron and calcium. If you go on a weeding binge and end up with a pile of dandelion roots, try making ersatz coffee. Clean the roots, then chop and roast them in a 300-degree oven until they're the same color you like your coffee beans. (Are you a French roast person or do you prefer an espresso roast?) Then, grind and prepare the roots as you would coffee beans, or combine 50 percent coffee and 50 percent dandelion root for New Orleans–style coffee. And then there's always dandelion wine . . .

Field garlic. Any plant that smells like onion or garlic is edible. There are some poisonous look-alikes, so be sure to smell before you taste. Take a piece of leaf, tear it, and sniff; the scent is unmistakable. Use the underground bulbs of field garlic as you would onions; or chop the leaves fine and use like chives. Bulbs can absorb any toxins in soil, so make sure to harvest field garlic away from any source of pollution. Field garlic is slightly darker than grass (and often grows in alongside it), has hollow leaves, and grows

Cattail pollen

Dandelion

Field garlic

Ginkgo nuts

Juneberry

to about a foot tall. You can harvest the leaves any time; bulbs will be best in spring and summer.

Ginkgo nuts. In early fall, female ginkgo trees produce stinky orange fruits, slightly smaller than a Ping-Pong ball. Inside the fruit (which smells like cheesy vomit) is a nut with a thin shell and a green center. Squeeze the fruit between two fingers to squirt out the nut. When you have enough, wash the nuts and lay them out on a baking sheet. Roast at 300°F for an hour. The nuts keep well if left in their shells for a few weeks in the fridge or a few months in the freezer. After shelling, you can either add gingko nuts to a soup or stir-fry, or sauté them in olive oil and salt them for a great snack with cold beer. The nuts are very tasty and full of protein.

Juneberry. Consider yourself lucky if you find Juneberry. The birds usually beat me to it and I can't blame them: this is a delicious fruit. The berries are slightly larger than cultivated blueberries and ripen from red to blue. (Any berry with a five-part crown, like a blueberry, is edible. They don't all taste good, but they're all safe to eat.) Juneberries ripen in July (go figure) and can be used in jellies and pies, or pop them directly into your mouth.

Bon appétit!

Foraging Rules

My friend Leda Meredith is a wild-edibles guru. She's taught the subject for years at various botanic gardens and parks, and publishes a newsletter on the subject. Here are her rules for foragers:

❖ *Never* eat anything unless you are 100 percent sure of its identity.

❖ Forage only where you have permission. (Or where you won't get caught if you don't have permission, like the back 40 of a very large park.)

❖ *Never* harvest within 50 feet of a busy road. Some plants absorb toxins from vehicle emissions.

❖ *Always* make sure you forage in a pesticide-free zone.

❖ Just because birds eat it doesn't mean it's safe for humans.

❖ Don't be greedy. Take no more than 25 percent of what's there; leave the rest for fellow foragers (animal and human), and to carry the crop into the future.

BASICS

Grow-Lights for Indoor Gardens

37

My New York City apartment is a fourth-floor studio with one window. The window looks across a 10-foot airshaft at another window (in another studio apartment, I suspect), so I have to either keep the curtain drawn 24/7 or keep my clothes on. The choice is clear. What is equally clear is that I couldn't live in a plantless apartment, so I have four kinds of grow-lights in this tiny studio.

There are just three things to understand about light: intensity, duration, and color.

Placing a plant too close to a light source isn't necessarily deadly, but it can definitely leave scars. A leaf will burn if it gets too hot; proper placement depends both on the plant and on the type of light you use. A good rule of thumb is if the leaf feels hot (not warm), it's too close to the bulb. If it starts to bubble and melt, it's *way* too close. When you install a grow-light, place the plant slightly farther from the light source than you think it belongs. (I'll give you a general rule for each kind of lightbulb.) Check periodically by feeling a leaf with your hands. If it feels and looks okay after 2 days, you can move it a little closer. Repeat this until you get the plant where you want it.

Intensity. Light intensity (brightness) is the single most important factor in growing plants indoors. Low light intensity produces leggy, weak plant growth and few or no flowers and fruit. Most people don't grasp how much less intense indoor light is than outdoor light. The light on a sunny windowsill is a mere fraction of what it would be outdoors. Fortunately, a lot of great houseplants are native to the rain-forest floor, and thus qualify as low- or medium-light plants.

Duration. This refers to the number of hours of light a plant gets per day. Because artificial light doesn't precisely duplicate sunlight, we compensate by giving plants more hours of light indoors than they would receive in their native habitat. We make up for reduced quality with increased quantity. But don't keep the lights on day and night. Plants need a period of uninterrupted darkness in order to flower, and different plants require different amounts of darkness. You don't need to worry about exactly how many hours of light most houseplants need. Remember that certain chemical processes take place only in darkness; a plant given light around the clock won't thrive indefinitely.

Color. Are you familiar with *roygbiv*? Red, orange, yellow, green, blue, indigo, violet: the colors of the visible light spectrum. Although the sun emits light in all these colors, light in the blue and red ranges is most important for plant growth. Flowering plants need orange/red light in order to bloom, and blue light promotes lush, compact growth for foliage plants.

The Choice Is Yours

There's a wide range of grow-lights available today. Some, such as incandescent bulbs, fluorescent tubes, and some compact fluorescent lightbulbs, fit into regular household fixtures. Others, such as High-Intensity Discharge and large compact fluorescent bulbs, come with their own fixtures. Before you choose, ask yourself

- ✿ What do I want to grow under the light?
- ✿ What style of light fixture will fit my space?
- ✿ What color of light is most agreeable to me?
- ✿ How much do I want to spend?

Fluorescent tubes are good for starting seeds and growing low-light plants, such as creeping fig *(Ficus pumila)* and many philodendrons. These lights are inexpensive both to buy and to use. They're efficient, giving off most of their energy as light and very little as heat, so you can place plants close to the tubes (4 to 6 inches) without worrying about foliage burn.

Fluorescent tubes come in standard lengths of 24 inches and 48 inches. Cool white tubes emit a bluish white light; warm bulbs produce a light with a reddish tint. You can use a combination of tubes in one fixture, or try full-spectrum fluorescent tubes, which emit a light whose color spectrum closely resembles the noonday sun. The Vita-Lite power twist is a full-spectrum light with an unusual molded shape that gives it greater surface area. This allows it to emit about 10 percent more light than a standard tube.

Fluorescent lights are most efficient when fitted with metal reflectors that direct light toward the plants. However, these give them a kind of stark, white, hospital-corridor look. No problem in a garage, basement, or studio workspace, but if you want a fixture in your living room, consider one that looks more like furniture. Line it with foil to increase reflected light, and you'll have a light with a finished look.

If you're starting trays of seeds, get yourself a light cart (one of my favorite Christmas presents ever). Several shelves with watertight trays give you lots of space for seed flats and small pots. The lights above the trays can be adjusted vertically, so you can keep them close to the seedlings as they emerge, promoting compact growth. (For more on this, see How to Start Seeds Indoors, page 14–15.)

Plants placed at the ends of the tubes receive less light than those at the center, so put your lowest-light plants at either end of the tubes. Replace fluorescent tubes every 18 months, as the gas escapes and oxidizes over time.

Small, compact fluorescent bulbs fit into incandescent fixtures and are perfect for spotlighting low-light specimens. Since the footprint is small, you can put one almost anywhere. Hang a single can fixture on the wall and aim it directly at your plant. These bulbs can be placed about 8 inches from the plant foliage.

This light cart has two levels of adjustable fluorescent tubes . . . perfect for starting seeds.

Incandescent grow-bulbs cast an attractive yellowish light.

Incandescent bulbs are less efficient than fluorescent; a lot of their energy is given off as heat rather than light. But don't write them off too quickly. They give off an attractive yellowish light that feels normal in a house, as opposed to the Miss Abbott's first-grade-classroom style of fluorescent tubes. And although they aren't models of efficiency, they're adequate for growing some low-light foliage plants indoors. If a corner of your apartment calls for a single specimen plant, try a cast iron plant (*Aspidistra elatior*) or a snake plant (*Sansevieria trifasciata*) under an incandescent grow-bulb.

A track-light fixture fitted with several incandescent bulbs is fine for low- and medium-light plants. Remember, these bulbs get hot. Keep plants at least 24 inches away from the light source.

High-Intensity Discharge (HID) lights are the gold standard when it comes to growing plants under artificial lights; I waited far too long to take the plunge. HID lights are the brightest available and you can grow just about anything under them. Place plants at least 12 inches from the bulbs. HID lights come in two varieties: metal halide and high-pressure sodium bulbs.

Metal halide (MH) bulbs give off light that looks slightly bluer than daylight. They promote compact, leafy growth and are a good choice for a living space because the light isn't freakishly colored. It is, however, *very* bright. Metal halide bulbs need to be replaced about once a year.

High-pressure sodium (HPS) bulbs last twice as long as metal halide lamps but cost slightly more. They promote flowers and fruit and their light is reddish yellow, giving everything a distinctly jaundiced look. Mine is relegated to the bathroom.

HID lights run off regular 110-volt household current but require special fixtures with ballasts. You can't just screw them into any old fixture: a metal halide bulb cannot be used in a high-pressure sodium fixture and vice versa. Fixtures are available that hold one of each kind of bulb, and the combination is a beautiful thing.

If you're tempted, try a small self-contained HID system with a 100-watt bulb. It's a plug-and-go setup and puts out enough light to illuminate a 3-foot-wide window with two shelves of plants.

Large compact fluorescent bulbs are excellent and less expensive than HID setups. They too require their own fixtures, which are about the same size as the small HID lights. The bulbs come in several colors (cool and warm). I prefer the cool for my living room. The warm isn't as strongly colored as an HPS bulb, but it's still too yellow for my taste. Light output is less intense than that of an HID lamp. You can grow a wide selection of medium- and low-light plants under these bulbs, adjusting the light intensity by manipulating the distance between lamp and plants. Prices range greatly from manageable to expensive, so shop around.

Mercury vapor light. For an isolated small spot of high light, try an Agrosun Power Gro Bulb. It's a mercury vapor light (150 watts) with a broader spectrum and more intense output than either an incandescent or a fluorescent grow bulb, but it has a smaller footprint than an HID fixture. It's self-ballasted and can be used in a floodlight-type lamp with a ceramic socket. This is another hot bulb, so keep your foliage about 24 inches from the fixture. Plus, it's bright in an "Argh! My eyes!" kind of way, so you're not going to want to use it in the living room unless you're giving a suspect the third degree. But, if your herbs need a boost, this bulb is for you.

Don't let lack of light cramp your style. Whether it's simple seed starting or coaxing high-light tropicals into bloom, you can accomplish wonders with a little ingenuity and a few dollars. Find your inner light — and grow something.

Compact fluorescent bulbs produce a daylight-quality light.

Shedding Some Light on Bulbs

Bulb Type	Best For...	Fixture Type	$–$$$	Consider
Fluorescent tubes	Starting seeds; low-light plants	Household or shop-light	$	Low light under ends of tubes
Compact fluorescent (small)	Low-light plants	Household	$	Convenient small footprint
Incandescent	Low-light plants	Household	$	Heat output
Compact fluorescent (large)	Medium-light plants	Specialized	$$	Nice quality of light
HID (MH and HPS)	High-light plants	Specialized	$$$	Pricy; color of HPS light is not flattering
Mercury vapor	Medium-light plants	Semi-specialized	$$	Heat output

A Garden for Feline Friends

38

Poor little kitties. They can't garden for themselves. They don't have tools. Or thumbs. But they sure like the sunshine, and they love to chew on green plants. In fact, they *need* to chew on green plants, so a garden for your cats can be both recreational and medicinal.

We've all seen our cats run outside, nibble some grass, then start heaving and backing up as if to walk out from under the emerging hairball. When a cat eats something he can't digest (bugs or hair, for instance), he needs to regurgitate to empty his stomacth. He eats the grass because it's an emetic; this behavior is entirely natural and not unhealthy. Many veterinarians

Kyra drinks from her cement pond after a grassy snack.

say cats eat grass for its folic acid, which cats need and can't get from meat. Additionally, grass can be a source of fiber, something lacking in many cat foods. If eaten in small amounts, grass aids in digestion. In larger amounts, it brings up lunch.

Cats also enjoy a little recreational herb use. (No one ever praises a cat for its admirable work ethic. Cats would much rather lie in the sun, twitching as they dream.) Several garden plants are alluring to cats, because of the essential oils they contain.

If you have 2 or 3 feet to spare in your garden and the area gets at least a half day of sun, why not plant something special for your cat? He may love it so much he'll leave the rest of your garden alone. Win-win, especially for daylily leaves, a feline delicacy. And while we're at it, let's really do it up right. Never mind a simple cat garden. Let's go for a fully landscaped cat sanctuary.

First, remember whose garden this is. If you're not going to be able to relax and relinquish control, you should skip this project. The plants in this garden are in for some tough love. They'll be chewed and rolled on, not groomed and deadheaded.

Cat Favorites

The plants I recommend do well in full to part sun. The more sun, the more flowers. Start them from seed or buy small plants. If you're going to start from seed, grow each type of plant in its own container. (See How to Start Seeds Indoors, pages 14–15).

Not Just for Summer

When autumn comes, cut back the catnip, catmint, and cat thyme and dry them for use over the winter. Make bundles of each herb, about an inch thick at the base, and fasten them together with an elastic band. Hang them upside down, somewhere warm, dry, and out of feline reach (dark is also good) and wait a few weeks. Your cats will enjoy these dried herbs as much as they relish the fresh ones.

Catmint (*Nepeta* x *faassenii,* aka *N. mussinii*)

A close relative of catnip (another *Nepeta*; see below), catmint contains a phytochemical (plant chemical) called nepetalactone, which is the magic ingredient that makes it popular with the feline crowd. Catmint gets to be about 18 inches tall, with silvery gray foliage and spikes of purple-blue flowers. Its flowers are more plentiful and showier than those of catnip. The cultivar 'Six Hills Giant' is particularly attractive and grows to about 4 feet tall. Zone 4.

Catnip *(Nepeta cataria)*

A member of the Mint family, catnip grows to 2 to 3 feet in height and is a spreading perennial. It has fragrant leaves and short spikes of small white or lavender flowers. Catnip contains even more nepetalactone than catmint. Regular pinching (or a quick trim after your cat has had a romp) will keep the plant bushy. If you find your cat destroying the catnip instead of just wrasslin' with it, consider planting some in an out-of-reach hanging basket and doling it out sprig by sprig. Zone 3.

Cat thyme *(Teucrium marum)*

Despite its name, cat thyme isn't a thyme, although it sure looks like one. With small, silvery green foliage and pink flowers, it's an attractive, drought-tolerant, aromatic plant, growing to about 12 inches in height. Cat thyme is highly fragrant; some humans don't like the smell, so sniff before you buy. Zone 7.

Catmint (*Nepeta* x *faassenii,* aka *N. mussinii*)

Catnip *(Nepeta cataria)*

Cat thyme *(Teucrium marum)*

Hops *(Humulus lupulus)*

Silver vine *(Actinidia polygama)*

Valerian *(Valeriana officinalis)*

Wheatgrass *(Triticum* species)

Hops *(Humulus lupulus)*

Although hops vine isn't traditionally considered a cat plant, our cat Kyra has a thing for beer, so I thought she might appreciate the hops flowers, which are not only pretty, but smell like the beverage itself. The leaf is attractive and this plant grows quickly, climbing 15 to 20 feet in a season. You'll need a female plant to get usable flowers. Zone 4.

Silver vine *(Actinidia polygama)*

This perennial grows to about 25 feet tall, with clusters of white flowers that produce orange fruit. (Silver vine is related to the kiwi (*A. deliciosa*), but its fruit isn't as delicious.) Its leaves contain the same phytochemical as that of valerian (actinidine, an alkaloid), which will get your kitty all riled up, then nicely calmed down. In Asia, leaves of this plant are used to sedate large cats in zoos. Zone 4.

Valerian *(Valeriana officinalis)*

Like catnip, this perennial initially energizes cats, but eventually the effect is sedative. It grows to 3 feet tall, has clumps of pink or white flowers, and sports large, cut leaves. The roots are used in medicinal preparations for humans, but cats chew on stems and leaves. Zone 4.

Wheatgrass (*Triticum* species), Oat grass (*Avena* species), or Ryegrass (*Lolium* species)

An emetic, wheatgrass will help your cat barf up those hairballs. Seeds sprout quickly (4 to 7 days), so it's easy to keep a fresh crop on hand. Cats consider the fresh sprouts a real delicacy. Annual.

Feline Garden Design

What else do cats like to do outdoors? Lie in the sun. Lie in the shade. Hunt. Eat. Drink. Sleep. Sounds good to me. Here are some design principles for gardening for the cats in your life, first the necessary elements, and then some suggestions on how to assemble them:

Sisko, hard at work.

✿ *Au naturel.* When you're planning a cat garden, leave a section unplanted. Cats love to roll around in the dirt (or mulch), covering themselves from head to toe in dust, then spend hours licking it off.

✿ **Hot rocks.** Find a flat rock or flagstone and place it slightly off-center in the garden, but smack dab in the sun where it will catch the sun's rays, soak up energy, and radiate heat all day — a warm and inviting spot for a cat siesta.

✿ **Shady retreat.** For balance, you should also provide a little shade. Using an adjoining wall, make a lean-to with a few boards. Or creatively stack some logs to create a cool spot where your cat can hide.

✿ **Refreshing water.** A water feature does double duty. Dig a shallow hole to hold a non-breakable dish of water, or use a small cement birdbath. Not only is water a refreshing beverage (as long as you refill it conscientiously) but it also attracts insects, which your cat will chase, catch, and eat. Oh boy.

✿ **Fountain.** Want to splurge? Use a small recycling fountain instead of a dish of water. Cats like the freshly aerated water, and the noise is pleasant in the garden.

✿ **Staggered heights.** Place taller plants — such as valerian or catnip, or hops vine trained up a trellis — at the back of the garden.

✿ **Less is more.** Catnip spreads, so a few small plants will suffice.

✿ **Filling in.** Use smaller plants like wheatgrass to fill in around the stone and the water feature.

✿ **Not for the birds.** Don't plant the cat garden near a bird feeder!

Buy Local:
Join a CSA

39

I get a lot of blank stares when I say I belong to a CSA. It's not a political party, it's not a sorority, there's no secret handshake. It stands for Community Supported Agriculture, and I'm not exaggerating when I say that it's changed my life.

Even those who've heard of CSAs sometimes suffer from the misconception that it's only for antisocial Luddites prepping for disaster by stocking up the pantry in their log cabins. Let me be clear: While I do have a very full pantry, I also eat meat with gusto, shave my legs, and

Rows of lettuce provide one of the first tastes of spring from the CSA.

am entirely dependent on wireless e-mail via my PDA. In other words, participating in a CSA doesn't mean you have to give up your standing pedicure appointment or any other modern-day conveniences.

Community Supported Agriculture helps local farmers by providing them with operating capital before their growing season starts, thus minimizing their risks and allowing them the freedom to grow a wide variety of interesting, unusual produce, rather than only what's guaranteed to sell best. Commercial tomato farmers grow varieties that can be picked green and shipped, arriving whole, unbruised, and, unfortunately, often tasteless. There are even genetically modified varieties of tomato whose raison d'être is an unusually long shelf life. Taste is beside the point. Well, the heirloom tomatoes from my CSA are fragile and sometimes a little cracked or spotted. They'd never make it to a large supermarket intact, and they don't always look flawless. But they are outrageously delicious.

So much of what we eat is produced on polluting factory farms, transported thousands of miles, and wrapped in tons of paper and plastic. The true environmental cost of this food is depressingly high. By eating local,

Caretaker Farm, located in Williamstown, Massachusetts, has been a CSA for more than a decade.

Buy Local: Join a CSA

Typical August pick-up at my NYC CSA.

How Local Is Local?

City CSAs usually have to look a little farther afield for a farmer, but they try to keep it within a 100-mile radius of the pickup point to minimize transportation costs and fuel use. Rural and suburban CSAs often have pickups at the farms and may include "pick-your-own" specials along with regular weekly shares.

Pick Your Own

TOMATOES — UNLIMITED
                YELLOW FLAGS
CHERRY TOMATOES — UNLIMITED BUT
                      WITHIN REASON
                      PINK FLAGS
COLLARDS — UNLIMITED
             PURPLE FLAGS
GREEN BEANS — UNLIMITED
                 RED FLAGS
PURPLE BEANS — UNLIMITED
                   BLUE FLAGS
RASPBERRIES — LIMIT 1 pint!
FOLLOW TAGS TO THE RIVER FIELD
FLOWERS   thyme
HERBS — basil, dill, tarragon
oregano, cilantro, parsley, lemon balm, chives

we do more than focus on fresh, seasonal produce. We support small farmers across the country and minimize the impact of agribusiness on the environment.

Here's how a CSA works: It's basically a variation of a food co-op. A group of interested individuals (like you) contract with a local farmer who agrees to provide weekly deliveries of seasonal produce; often the produce is organic, but not always. The farmer sets a price per share, which members pay in advance of the growing season. This gives the farmer capital up front for seeds, labor, and equipment. Together, farmer and members form a CSA.

Each CSA member picks up produce every week of the season (the length of which varies). Some groups sell larger, family shares and half shares for couples or individuals. I have no problem handling a full share with just Michael and me. (Remember my very well-stocked pantry?)

You never know exactly what your share will include, but the produce will always be fresh and in season. In other words, you won't be getting garlic scapes in November or hot peppers in June. It's amazing how quickly

seasonal eating puts you in touch with the world around you. The first greens of spring are a special event, just as ratatouille in August is reason to rejoice. It feels so right to be eating what's growing around us right now!

By paying in advance, you assume some risk. If a crop fails (as my farmer's butternut squash did last year), you're out of luck. And most CSAs ask their members to volunteer a few hours per season. There are also potluck suppers and farm visits, and many groups offer fruit shares, flower shares, and cheese, meat, poultry, egg, and honey deliveries. You'll soon find yourself part of a community with a common interest in healthy, delicious, fresh food.

Which is a good thing, because you're going to need help figuring out what to do with the cornucopia of cucumbers and the overflow of apples. CSAs put out weekly newsletters with recipe suggestions to tell you what to do with your celeriac, tomatillos, and the aforementioned garlic scapes. Surf the Net, ask your friends, read cookbooks. Get creative.

Not being much of a vegetable person,* I had to stretch to figure out how to use these new foods. There's no denying that eating this way takes a little more work. The food isn't wrapped in plastic, it's not waxed, most of it is dirty, and there's an occasional spider. But the rewards go far beyond good taste and good health; the satisfaction is deep. If I can do it, so can you, and here are a few favorite recipes to start you on your way. Even though most of us don't have the wherewithal to be full-scale farmers, there's no reason we can't enjoy fresh, interesting food year-round.

To find a CSA near you, see Resources in the appendix.

*This falls into the category of gross understatement. As a child I swallowed my peas like pills, in groups of 10 or 12 so I wouldn't have to touch the mushy insides. All beans were my enemies, and the mere smell of brussel sprouts made me nauseous. Still does.

Apple-Chipotle Chutney

1 ½ pounds apples, cored and chopped (not peeled)
1 garlic clove, minced
1 tablespoon fresh ginger root, finely chopped
½ cup orange juice
1 teaspoon ground cinnamon
1 teaspoon whole cloves
1 teaspoon kosher salt
1 cup honey
1 cup cider vinegar
1 tablespoon chopped chipotle peppers in adobo sauce
(2, if you like it spicy and smoky!)

Combine all ingredients in a large, heavy saucepan and bring it to a boil. Lower heat to a simmer and cook uncovered for 1 hour, stirring occasionally.

Tzatziki

I like my tzatziki thick, so I use goat's yogurt or let regular yogurt drip overnight through a cheese strainer. If you prefer a softer consistency, use regular yogurt straight out of the container.

1 cup plain, unsweetened, unflavored yogurt
2 garlic cloves, minced
1 cucumber, peeled and shredded
1 tablespoon lemon juice
Salt and pepper to taste

Stir all ingredients together and serve with crusty bread or on crackers for a cool, summer appetizer.

Ratatouille (aka Summer in a Jar)

Olive Oil
1 large onion, chopped
2 bell peppers (any color), chopped
2 garlic cloves, minced
3 large tomatoes, chopped
1 large (or two small) eggplant, sliced
2 zucchini or summer squash, sliced
Salt, pepper, basil, and rosemary to taste

Sauté onion, peppers, and garlic in oil until soft. Add eggplant and zucchini (and perhaps a little more oil!) and continue to cook until the vegetables soften and darken. You're not frying the vegetables, but rather letting them stew together to fuse the flavors. Add tomatoes, salt and pepper, and herbs, and cook 30 to 45 minutes. Tweak seasoning before serving.

It Ain't Just Dirt: Improve Your Garden Soil

40

What's your soil like? Hard as cement, insanely rocky, or fluffy and light like a fairy garden? This will determine which tools you need, and it will also prepare you mentally for the task at hand. *Por ejemplo,* my parents' soil is so fabulous that I barely need a shovel; at my house (Rock City, PA) I can't plant a petunia without a pickax. Go outside, put a shovel in the ground, and push it in as far as you can. Did you get 8" to 10" down without resistance? (Congratulations!) Did you hit a rock at 4"? (Join the club.) Did you have to jump on the top of the shovel to make it penetrate even 2"? (Choose another spot.)

The texture of soil is referred to as *tilth*. There are three basic categories, plus the inevitable subcategories.

- ❀ **Clay soils** are heavy, wet, slow to drain, and difficult to dig.
- ❀ **Sandy soils** are heavy, dry, quick-draining, and easy to dig, and they don't retain nutrients.
- ❀ **Loamy soils** are perfect and lovely, easy to dig and full of nutrients.
- ❀ **Mixtures.** There are also sandy loams, sandy clays, loamy clays, clayey loams, and so on.

Miraculously, there's a magic remedy for any soil with a less than perfect tilth, and that's compost. Add compost to a clay soil and it lightens it up and improves drainage. Compost in a sandy soil helps it retain both water and nutrients and drain more slowly. And, of course, compost adds nutrients to any soil.

Scalable Composting: No Garden Left Behind

You can begin composting on almost any scale. I'm reluctant to compost food leftovers because of the wildlife that shares our two Pennsylvania acres. If bears destroy the hummingbird feeders to get to the sugar water, I can imagine what they'd do to get to dinner scraps in a compost bin. My compost pile consists of oak and beech leaves, as well as recycled soil from annual garden containers. It's literally a pile in the woods that I stir a couple of times per season. (You could also compost leaves in a cage made of fencing material.) For very little work I'm rewarded with crumbly leaf mold that *greatly* improves the tilth of my soil.

If you're interested in going further, consider making or buying a compost bin. County Extension offices and botanic gardens often give away basic bins and offer free classes on composting. Fancier, spinning compost bins eliminate the need for stirring and speed the transformation from leftovers to compost.

Let's start simple. Using whatever material is handy (cinder blocks, plastic sheeting, metal scraps), construct a square 4 to 6 feet wide, and 3 feet tall. A cover will keep out marauding animals, but isn't necessary for the

To Pee or Not to Pee

In any conversation about compost, someone asks if it's true that peeing on a compost pile speeds up decomposition. Well, yes, it does. A little. The best thing you can do to accelerate decomposition is to keep the pile wet and regularly turned for good aeration. Although it's true that pee is a source of nitrogen, more effective sources include lawn clippings and manure. The surprise benefit of peeing on your compost pile (and only if you have sufficient privacy in your garden!) is that it's an excellent pest deterrent. Just as many mammals mark their territory, you can mark your compost pile. It's an effective way of letting Mr. Raccoon know there's a much bigger dog around.

Enclosed compost bins keep out animals.

217

Composted Manure

You probably haven't spent a lot of time thinking about the characteristics of various manures. Am I right? Well, there's a first time for everything. Composted manure is simply manure that has been allowed to decompose, which makes it a better choice for direct garden application for several reasons:

❖ It won't stink.

❖ Any weed seeds or bad fungi will have been killed.

❖ It won't burn your plants' roots. The nutrients in raw manure are highly soluble; they are quickly leached from the soil and can damage both the plants and the soil food web. Composted manure releases its nutrients into the soil slowly.

composting process itself. In the bin, alternate layers of organic material like table scraps, coffee grounds, tea bags, leaves, grass clippings, and even weeds with layers of soil and manure. Do *not* include meat, fish, or chicken scraps or bones; pet poop is also a no-no. Water the pile occasionally in summer and turn it with a garden fork once a week to mix it up and keep decomposition even. During decomposition, the temperature at the center of the pile will get hot enough to kill weed seeds.

As the pile decomposes, individual pieces become smaller, the volume of compost decreases, and the pile darkens in color. You'll notice when decomposition slows and the pile cools; then earthworms and other soil organisms move in, doing their part to break down the compost. Chemical accelerators are unnecessary. They're basically freeze-dried microorganisms, which are all over your compost anyway. It should take about a year to get usable compost; the process will be slower if you include woody material (branches, mulch chips) in the pile. If you're in a hurry, you can dig out some finished compost from the bottom of the pile.

If you're in an urban or suburban area, consider a compost tumbler. It doesn't take up too much space and keeps the compost out of sight. It can sit peacefully in an unused corner of your yard or deck. Plus, turning the tumbler is easier than turning a pile with a pitchfork, and you'll get faster decomposition. City life is all about speed!

If you get hooked, you can tweak your system by gauging the carbon-to-nitrogen ratio, measuring and regulating the temperature at the center of the pile, and buying fancy aerator tools. But even the simplest pile of composted leaves will markedly improve your soil, and thereby your garden.

This Is a Test

Now for a quick soil test. Kits are available at garden centers, big box stores, and via mail order. The test is simple and involves mixing "several small soil samples" (try to say that five times fast) with distilled water and various chemicals. You then compare the results of each test to a color chart to determine the soil pH and basic nutrient content. Kits are inexpensive and contain everything you need except the soil and water. By testing, you'll know exactly how to amend the soil to give your garden a good start.

My soil is acid, as is much of the garden soil in the United States. This means it has a pH of less than 7.0. The pH scale goes from 0 to 14: 0 is the most acidic and 14 is the most basic (or alkaline). Soils in the Southwest tend to have a basic/alkaline pH. Some plants have specific pH requirements, but most do well within a pH range of 5.5 to 7.5. If your pH is much different from this, test again. If it's still way off, try amending your soil to correct the pH. Making a *big* change to the pH of your soil (for example, from 7.0 to 5.5) isn't easy. Each number indicates a tenfold difference in acidity. (pH is calculated on a logarithmic scale.) A soil with a pH of 6.0 is ten times more acidic than a soil with a pH of 7.0. You can tweak the acidity/alkalinity with soil amendments, but the best thing to do is plant things that are appropriate for the soil pH you already have. The second best thing is to use organic amendments and minerals regularly to improve your soil over time. To acidify your soil, add acidic organic matter like peat or pine needles. To make your soil more alkaline, add lime.

Food for Thought: Testing for the Big Three

Any soil kit will also test for three macronutrients: nitrogen (N), phosphorus (P), and potassium (K). These nutrients are essential for healthy plant growth and are contained in most commercial fertilizers. Your test will tell you if you have a dearth of any of these elements. If your soil is deficient, you have several choices. You can either amend it with organic material, such as humus, peat, leaf mold, or compost, or use synthetic or organic fertilizers to improve the nutrient concentration specifically for the plant you're planting.

If you're digging a mixed border, go ahead and add organic material throughout the bed. There are no existing plants to disturb, so you can dig it in deep and evenly. Adding organic matter improves both the tilth and the nutrient content of your soil. Here are some tried-and-true organic amendments:

Acid-Loving Natives

Many native woodland plants are what we call acid-loving. They require a soil with a pH of 4.5 to 5.5. Rhododendrons, azaleas, mountain laurels, sweet fern, and blueberries are just a few of the wonderful plants that need an extra-acid soil. The soil pH affects which nutrients are available to the plants growing in it, and acid-loving plants require different levels of nutrients than non-acid-loving plants. You can use a special acid plant food to grow these plants in a soil with normal acidity.

You can add soil amendments to planting holes before setting in your plants.

For nitrogen, add composted manure. Both cow manure and chicken manure are good, but chicken is more potent than cow, so follow the recommended proportions carefully. An overapplication of manure can burn plant roots.

For phosphorus, dig in some bonemeal. This will also slightly raise the pH of the soil.

For potassium, add wood ashes or greensand (a silica-based material containing potassium and nitrogen). If you heat with a wood stove in winter, save the ashes and recycle them in the garden.

Dig In

Spread the soil amendments on top of your soil and dig them into the bed to a depth of about 6 inches. If you do the whole bed at once, you'll be ready to plant the rest of the garden whenever you want.

On the other hand, if you're adding to an existing garden, it's easier to add fertilizer or organic matter to only the immediate growing area. You can

The Scoop on Fertilizers

Any fertilizer you buy has three numbers on the label. They refer to nitrogen, phosphorus, and potassium, in that order. The numbers indicate the percentage (by weight) of the fertilizer that is made up of each element. Additional info is on the back label. A balanced fertilizer shows three equal numbers: 5-5-5, 10-10-10, 15-15-15, for example. Specialized fertilizers deliver higher concentrations of one element or another: say, 7-9-11 or 10-60-10.

Fertilizers can be water soluble or granular. Water-soluble fertilizers are easier to deliver to existing plants. You just feed the plant when you water, with a hose-end sprayer or by inserting a fertilizer solution into the irrigation lineup (see Irrigation

Systems 101, page 121). A hose-end sprayer is a sprayer that attaches to the end of your hose. It can be used to apply fertilizers, insecticides, weedkillers, etc. It's a good idea to keep separate sprayers for different substances. Imagine the tragedy of applying fertilizer to your tomatoes with a sprayer that contains the remnants of a weedkiller. Bye-bye tasty fruit!

Granular fertilizers work best added to the soil when you're planting something. Time-release granules can be added to the bottom of the planting hole; most dissolve over a 6- to 9-month period. In following years, you'll scratch additional applications of granular fertilizers into the soil around the plant or use a water-soluble plant food.

It Ain't Just Dirt

use a balanced fertilizer, which gives you equal parts nitrogen, phosphorus, and potassium, or apply a fertilizer that gives you more of one or the other, depending on what your soil test tells you that you need.

Much Ado about Mulch

Now it's time to mulch. Organic mulch serves several purposes. It slows the loss of moisture from the soil by evaporation. It cuts down on weed germination, still allowing for penetration of air, water, and nutrients. As mulch biodegrades it adds organic matter to the soil, improving both texture and nutrient content. Plus, it looks nice. Usually.

Lay a 2- to 3-inch layer of mulch around your trees, leaving a space around the trunk.

In the name of Garden Aesthetics, I *beg* you, never, ever buy or use dyed red mulch! It's hideously ugly and a color not found in nature. It is *not* natural redwood. (Seriously, redwood trees don't have *red wood*. Redwood trees make a good, fibrous mulch, which actually is tawny brown.) Gardening is all about celebrating nature, so why would you want to add a lot of red-dye-#-whatever to your garden beds? Remember, mulch biodegrades and becomes part of the soil food web. Why add a grotesque red chemical to the food chain? I tell my students that if I ever catch them using red mulch I'll give them an F. Obviously, that would be an empty threat here, but you get my point.

Go for the natural colors of shredded pine or cedar; nuggets are also fine. If you're gardening on a slope, or simply want a heavier mulch that won't blow away, use a hardwood mulch. Or if you feel like experimenting, try cocoa hulls. They biodegrade more quickly than pine, cedar, or hardwood, so you get only a single season out of them, but the color is neutral and the smell is chocolaty delicious. That's no joke.

To mulch around a tree, spread a 2- to 3-inch layer of mulch over the soil, leaving a small space around the trunk of the tree. Do not mound the mulch to form a mountain around the trunk; this inhibits air exchange through the bark and roots. We professionals call these "mulch volcanoes." When we see them we point and laugh. I encourage you to do the same.

Winterize!

Alas, the cold rains of October have arrived. A hot and humid September lulled me into believing that *this time,* summer would last forever. Then came October, and with it . . . the rains.

Leaves turn brown and the garden looks pathetic and accusing, except for the regal monkshood (*Aconitum carmichaelii,* Zone 3), which stands 5 feet tall and scoffs at the cold and wet. Despite this brave show, I must admit it's time to prepare the garden for winter.

I start by taking a slow walk around the garden, making notes (real notes, not mental notes) about what should be divided and moved. I like to do this in fall for several reasons. First, my plants will come up in spring looking whole, rather than like pie wedges (see Multiply Your Plants by Dividing, page 185). Also, in fall I can see how big things have gotten and where I have holes to fill. I've learned all too well from past experience that by late April, I won't have a clue.

Once temperatures drop reliably into the 60s and 50s, feel free to divide and transplant. Cooler temperatures make it easier for a plant to recuperate from the trauma of surgery. Remember, recent transplants need extra water, and fall rains will assist you in this task.

After the first frost, pull up the annuals that have turned to mush. Thank them as you toss them on the compost pile — they bloomed long and hard for you, and you appreciate it.

Dig up dahlia tubers and hang them for a few days to let them dry.

Gee . . . What's a Geophyte?

There's a group of plants that grow from underground storage tissue rather than from a network of roots. Called *geophytes,* these include bulbs, corms, tubers, rhizomes, and more. The nice thing is that if you're not sure exactly which type of geophyte you're talking about, you can simply call it a geophyte and everyone will be impressed because it's such a fancy word.

If you grew tender geophytes in the garden this year (like *Caladium, Canna,* and *Colocasia*), then dig them up to overwinter. The first time I did this successfully was entirely accidental, which tells you how easy the process is.

Dig up tubers (or bulbs or corms) and shake off the soil. You should be able to rub off the attached stems and leaves; they will have died back after the frost. Let the tubers dry for a few days, then put them in a plastic bag of peat moss, pushing each tuber well into the moss. Put the bag in a cool, dark place, where temperatures will stay above freezing, and that's about it. Once a month, check the tubers for mold or shriveling. If they feel dry and wrinkly, spray them with water from a mister bottle but don't saturate. If they're

Dig up your caladiums to overwinter them as dormant geophytes.

Once your perennials have been hit by a frost, cut them back to about 2 to 3 inches tall.

moldy, cut out the soft spots and remove the tubers (or bulbs or corms) from the bag to dry for a few days. Caladiums should be stored warmer than most other tender bulbs, at 50° to 60°F.

When spring comes, take a look at the tubers. You may already see some green sprouts. Whether or not that's the case, you can plant them outside as soon as it's warm enough. Different tender geophytes grow best at different temperatures, so check the recommendations for whatever you're planting. For example, caladiums like it warm, so when temperatures reach the 70s, replant the tubers, and voilà! You have successfully overwintered.

If you grow geophytes in containers, overwintering is even easier. Cut back the foliage and move the containers into a dark, frost-free place. Once a month, give each pot a little water. Check in the spring, and more likely than not, growth will have started on its own. When it's warm enough, move the containers outside and start watering normally.

What to Do with Those Perennials and Grasses

Some perennials die back after a frost or two; some last till a hard freeze. Either way, try to cut back the garden before snow comes. A general rule is to cut back perennials to 2 or 3 inches above the ground, leaving only stubs.

There may be some plants you'd like to leave up for winter interest. The flowers of many ornamental grasses look lovely with a dusting of snow, waving in a winter wind. The wide, flat flowers of *Sedum* 'Autumn Joy' dry to a rich rusty brown and look like a dried flower arrangement in the garden. If you decide to leave some black-eyed Susans (*Rudbeckia fulgida*) standing, do it only in moderation. Black-eyed Susan is a terrific plant but it seeds so freely that in no time you'll have nothing but these yellow flowers in your garden.

Once the garden is cut back, it's time to plant spring bulbs. (See Forcing Spring Bulbs, page 2). Do this while you can still see the stubs of the perennials, so you don't inadvertently cut into anything, destroying its root system. In other words, plant bulbs before you mulch.

Dahlias are also worth keeping, but they should be handled differently. These are tuberous roots, and there's a growing bud at the base of each stem. You don't want to remove the stems completely when you're storing dahlias for the winter; you need the bud for next year's growth.

just hangin' out

Gently dig the whole bundle of tubers out of the ground. Cut off most of each stem, leaving an inch or two, then hang the tubers upside down for a few days so any water can drain from the stem bases.

cut ups

Divide each tuber by cutting through it vertically with a sharp knife, making sure each piece of tuber has a piece of stem attached. Let the pieces dry for a few days, then bury them in a bag of peat moss or sand and treat them as you would the bulbs, corms, and tubers above. P.S. Smell the dahlia roots before putting them away for the winter. They have a delicious, spicy scent.

Got Mulch?

You can purchase bagged mulch, or, since most of us have leaves a-plenty this time of year, use them as a freebie. Run a lawn mower over your leaf pile to chop up the leaves. This makes them fluffier and faster to biodegrade, and keeps them from forming slick mats of wet heaviness.

An Ounce of Protection

Mulch? You're thinking, "But I already mulched in the spring!" Yes, but now it's time for *winter mulch*. Spread the mulch thickly over everything, covering the stubby ends of all those perennials, giving them a nice warm blanket for protection. A 4-inch layer of mulch will keep perennial roots from heaving as the ground repeatedly freezes and thaws during the winter.

Some plants, especially evergreens, need extra protection from harsh winter winds. Because they hold their leaves (and needles), these plants continue to transpire (release moisture) in winter, albeit at a reduced rate. Winter winds wick moisture out of leaves, and if the ground is frozen, plants may not be able to replace the water they lose. Needles and leaves turn brown as they dry out; this is called *desiccation*.

There are several things you can do to protect your plants. Broadleaf evergreens (rhododendrons, hollies, and mountain laurels, for example) are most severely affected. Spray their leaves with an antidesiccant in late fall: this creates a barrier that slows the loss of water from the leaves. Reapply after heavy rains.

Above: Spread a 3" to 4" layer of mulch over your entire garden as winter protection.

Right: Spray holly with an antidesiccant in late fall to protect it over winter.

Or, wrap the tree or shrub in burlap to give it physical protection from drying winds. If you're growing in movable containers, bring them to a sheltered spot up against a building wall. Additionally, if the temp goes above 45 degrees, it's a good idea to water any evergreen.

If you live where there's lots of ice and snow, you may have noticed that it collects on the roof and has a tendency to slide off every now and then, crushing everything in its path. If someone was shortsighted in designing your garden and placed a tree or a shrub in the path of this avalanche, you can do one of three things:

✿ Move the tree or shrub.

✿ Wrap the plant in burlap to hold it together, so heavy snow won't lodge in the crotches and break off branches.

✿ Place a stiff sandwich board over the shrub (probably not practical for a tree) so that any falling snow or ice hits the board and slides off onto the ground.

If you're growing shrubs or trees in containers, you may need to give the root-balls some extra protection. Remember, plants in the ground have a great volume of soil insulating their roots. In a container, there's much less soil protecting the root-ball, and roots may get too cold, thus killing the plant. Encase a round pot in a few layers of bubble wrap; tape sheets of Styrofoam insulation to the walls of a rectangular container. For a decorative touch (and to hide the bubble wrap), wrap the whole thing in burlap, tied with a pretty ribbon.

Once the garden is fully winterized, call your travel agent and buy yourself some time on a tropical beach. Your plants won't need you until spring.

The rootball of this dwarf Alberta spruce is protected and ready for winter.

Winter
Window Boxes

42

I'm the first to admit that I don't feel much like gardening when it's raining, snowing, sleeting, or any combination of the above. Freezing temps, gray days, wet feet, all of these things make me want to stay inside and thumb through plant catalogs. But *this* is the time of year when we *need* something bright in the garden: to perk us up, give us horticultural encouragement, and remind us that tomorrow is another day.

Plant a winter window box and you'll have color in the garden amid the snow and ice. There are two kinds of winter plantings to consider: cut branches and living plants. Both make a nice contrast to the gray of winter.

Let's start with the less familiar: boughs and berries. People in my business use the phrase "bough-and-berry" as a verb.

Gardener #1: Have you been busy?

Gardener #2: (wearily) Yeah, I boughed-and-berried all week.

OR

Gardener #1: Have you put your gardens to bed yet?

Gardener #2: Well, I still have to bough-and-berry.

Alive and Well All Winter

If you'd like to plant a living evergreen display, start with a frost-proof container. Most terra-cotta will crack if planted and left outside over the winter. As the moisture in the clay freezes and thaws, it expands and contracts, which ordinary clay can't tolerate. Cast iron, wood, and fiberglass work better. If you must have terra-cotta, paint it inside and out with several coats of a water-seal product before planting.

Choose a variety of evergreen plants: contrasting textures and colors that please you. Remember "thriller, filler, and spiller" (When It Comes to the Plants, page 32)?

Your hardiness zone determines what will be evergreen in your container. Black mondo grass is evergreen in Zone 7, but not necessarily in Zone 4. Do a little research before buying plants. And remember, plants in containers are more vulnerable to cold, having limited soil to insulate their root-balls. To be safe, select plants that are hardy to one or two zones colder than where you live.

Create a Winter Arrangement

If you have a window box that held annuals over the summer and is now empty, decorate it with a combination of cut branches. Broadleaf and needle evergreens, berries, and unusual bare branches will look festive for months. A florist should carry these materials, or you could always grab your pruners and head out into the woods!

Start with large evergreen branches. White pine is long-lasting and feathery soft. Juniper has loads of blue berries and branches shaped like a fox tail. Blue spruce has a wonderful gray-blue color and stiff form. Broadleaf evergreens are shiny, with a range of leaf shapes, colors, and sizes, from itty-bitty boxwood to magnificent magnolia. (Magnolia branches also have large, decorative cones on the ends.)

toe the line

Place a line of your largest evergreen branches down the center of the box. This creates a backdrop against which the colorful berries and bark will be displayed; you'll be filling it in from both sides. Remember, these boxes will be looked at from indoors and out, so you want to make sure the view is lovely from both.

compound interest

On either side of the evergreen backdrop, stick interesting branches into the soil. Consider yellowish, twisting willow branches, red-twig dogwood, or the contorted limbs of Harry Lauder's walking stick.

berry pretty

Choose berries to complete the picture: red winterberry, yellow and orange bittersweet, pink rose hips. Place these in between the branches, where the berries will show up nicely against the green backdrop. Accessorize with pinecones, some miniature gourds, or perhaps white pin lights or a few holiday ornaments. The personal touches are up to you.

Creating
a Garden
Refuge

43

I put off writing this chapter for a long time, because I realized that when I wrote it the book would be done, and I didn't want it to be over. Which relates to the project title: There comes a time when you have to stop working and relax, to put down the trowel and find refuge in the garden. You've worked hard and it's time to enjoy the flowers of your labor.

The truth is, a garden is never finished. There will always be new plants to try, old plants to divide, seedlings to transplant. Each season calls for new annuals,

or you may just wake up one day and want something different. Remember: All work and no play makes Jack a dull gardener.

Surely you've imagined yourself relaxing in the garden, stretched out on a chaise or enjoying dinner alfresco. Let the style of your garden refuge be as personal as your choice of plants.

Some people like the smooth surface of aged teak, but I've always had a thing for 1950s outdoor metal furniture. There's something about it that grabs me: sturdy, colorful, kitschy, practical. I started out with a pair of yellow bouncy chairs, then added two pairs of green ones and a round table with an umbrella. Arranged around the fire pit and the flagstone patio, this gave us an outdoor room. But something was missing. A glider. A green, metal, couch-sized glider. Fifty dollars at a summer flea market. Now I can really lie back and relax, if Sisko will give up the spot.

How do you unwind? Do you like to be alone, hidden from the world? A solitary chair by a stream is a perfect spot to read. The white noise of rushing water makes it easy to concentrate.

Perhaps you'd like a platform perched on a wooded hill, where you can look out over all that surrounds you. A glass of wine, a skein of yarn, and you're golden.

There's something about the sound of water that soothes even the most stressed-out, overworked air traffic controller. Just think what it will do for *your* garden!

A classic marshmallow roast, surrounded by tiki torches, in our Pennsylvania refuge.

Me, I want a spot in the sun where I can lie down with my cats. The gentle back and forth of a glider or the hammock is a bonus.

The point is that how you relax makes a big difference in how you plan a garden refuge. Maybe you fall into one of these categories. Maybe you fall into more than one. Mix and match if you like; you make the rules.

The Entertainer

Nothing makes you happier than an evening with friends. Light up the tiki torches, chill the white wine, and put a huge pot of water on the barbecue to boil. We're having corn on the cob! Later it'll be s'mores around the fire pit and maybe someone will break out a guitar. If that's your idea of a perfect evening, your garden refuge needs to include outdoor dining space. Seating for six with enough flat space for a table and a grill, along with an umbrella to protect you from hot sun or drizzle, will make this space usable on any kind of warm day.

The Loner

When work is over, you throw yourself into a chair on the deck or lawn with a good book. No television, no music, just the sound of the wind in the trees and the chirp of the peepers. A kerosene lamp on a tree stump gives you enough light to read by once it's dark. Make sure the chair is comfy and give yourself a stool to rest your weary feet. Consider planting something to

In this back courtyard garden, the city traffic seems miles away.

screen you from a nosy neighbor who might stop by uninvited: a large clump of ornamental grass is just big enough to hide you from view.

The Romantic

Maybe you and your sidekick want somewhere you can sit, trade stories about the day, open a few bottles of homebrew, and snack on some popcorn. It might even be nice to listen to a little music on a warm evening. Make room in your garden for two Adirondack chairs, perhaps at a curve in the border with a view of the hummingbird garden, or somewhere you can watch the cats roll in the catnip. A cooler for the beer, a dock for the iPod, and you're set.

The Yogi

Life in the city can be anything but relaxing. If you crave a place above the fray where you can slow the pace, stretch, and maybe even meditate, you can have it without a lot of space. The swish of bamboo in the wind or the gurgle of a small fountain can block the noise of the traffic on the street below. Leave room among your containers to spread a yoga mat and offer sun salutations directly to the sky above. Or, if you're not into meditation, find a quiet spot to catch up on correspondence, electronic or otherwise. If it's a Wi-Fi hot spot, even better.

The Family Guy/Gal

For you, fun time is family time. Do your kids like a sandbox? Do they have a jungle gym? Do you like to snuggle up together in the hammock to read a story? A family spot should be soft underfoot: lawn, moss, anything spongy and green. Don't situate it near a water garden (where balls can splash) or a rose collection (sharp thorns). Give the kids someplace to play where they can't hurt anything and nothing can hurt them. Make sure there's enough space for everyone (no fighting, no biting) and try to include both sun and shade.

The Artist

Your urge to create extends beyond the garden and a beautiful view stimulates you. Even a small deck offers enough space to set up an easel or settle in with your journal. Whatever your craft, you'll find the fresh air energizing. And the shimmer of a dragonfly's wing may inspire a painting or poem unlike anything you could write indoors. Give yourself room to create, with a little extra space for a cool beverage on the side.

The Gamer

Don't get the wrong idea: Playstations and Xboxes are banned from my garden. There are, however, plenty of games that bring people together and actually encourage conversation, maybe even allow for a little friendly competition. You can find an old croquet set at a yardsale, and if a few wickets are missing, make replacements from heavy-gauge wire. There's bocce ball, badminton, and even kubb. (It's rumored to be a Viking game. Google it.) You can play with two or you can play with teams. The important thing is to play.

Promise me one thing: that you'll relax and enjoy what you've labored so diligently to create. You didn't plant this garden to impress the neighbors. (Well, not *just* to impress the neighbors.) You did it to create a personal green space where you can revel in the glory of nature. It's entirely possible that while you're sitting there with your feet up, you'll notice a patch of garden that needs weeding or some annuals that need deadheading. Put it off till tomorrow. I give you permission.

USDA Hardiness Zone Map

The United States Department of Agriculture (USDA) created this map to give gardeners a helpful tool for selecting and cultivating plants. The map divides North America into 11 zones based on each area's average minimum winter temperature. Zone 1 is the coldest and Zone 11 the warmest. Recently, the zones were further divided into A and B, with A being the colder portion. To locate your zone, refer to the map here, or use the Zone Finder on the National Gardening Association's Web site (see Resources), which identifies zones by zipcode.

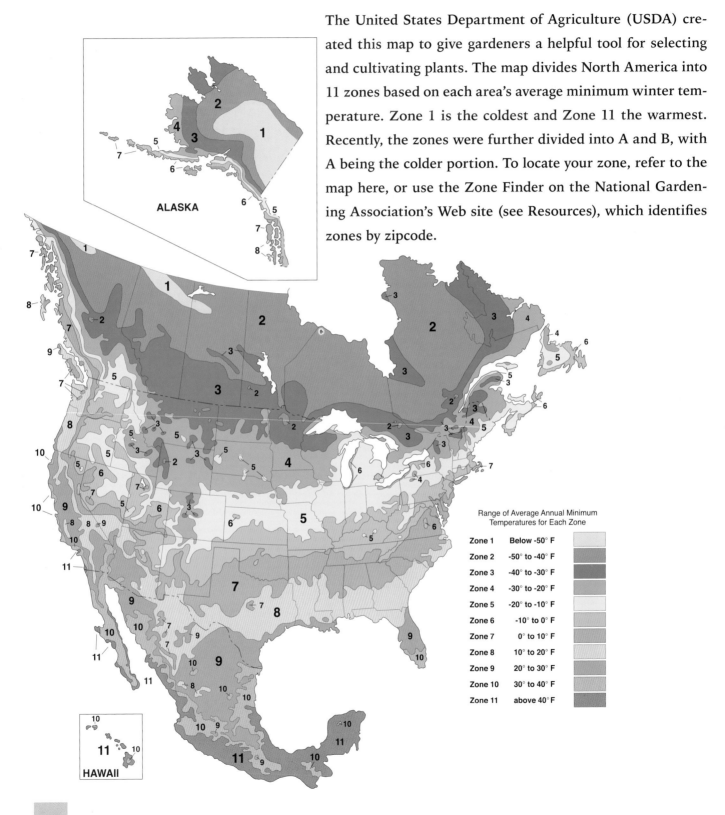

ALASKA

HAWAII

Range of Average Annual Minimum
Temperatures for Each Zone

Zone 1	Below -50° F
Zone 2	-50° to -40° F
Zone 3	-40° to -30° F
Zone 4	-30° to -20° F
Zone 5	-20° to -10° F
Zone 6	-10° to 0° F
Zone 7	0° to 10° F
Zone 8	10° to 20° F
Zone 9	20° to 30° F
Zone 10	30° to 40° F
Zone 11	above 40° F

Resources

Internet Resources

Community gardening

www.communitygarden.org

Community Supported Agriculture

www.nal.usda.gov/afsic/csa

Deerproofing

www.dancinggardenmirrors.com

Hummingbirds

www.hummingbirds.net/map.html

Invasive plants

www.invasiveplants.net

National Gardening Association

www.garden.org

Organic pest controls

www.greenmethods.com

Plant a Row for the Hungry

877-492-2727

www.gardenwriters.org/Par

Mentioned in Text

Lowenfels, Jeff, and Wayne Lewis. *Teaming With Microbes: A Gardener's Guide to the Soil Food Web* (Timber, 2006)

Rushing, Felder. *Scarecrows: Making Harvest Figures and Other Yard Folks* (Storey, 1998)

Thompson, Robert Farris. *Flash of the Spirit: African & Afro-American Art & Philosophy* (Vintage Books, 1984)

Bulb Suppliers

Brent and Becky's Bulbs

877.661.2852

www.brentandbeckysbulbs.com

Dutch Gardens

888.821.0448

www.dutchgardens.com

K. Van Bourgondien & Sons, Inc.

800.622.9959

www.dutchbulbs.com

Additional Photography Credits

© Henry W. Art: 20 second down, 97 top, 176 top; © David Cavagnaro: 151 top, 152 bottom; © cfgphoto.com: 102 right, 195 middle; © Joseph De Sciose: 25, 126, 129, 174 second down; © Catriona Tudor Erler: 162 bottom; © Derek Fell: 76, 85 second down, 138 top, 139 bottom, 194 top, 195 top, 226 right, 230 top; © judywhite/Gardenphotos.com: 85 third down; © Garden Picture Library: Marie O'Hara 85 bottom, John Glover 103 middle, Jo Whitworth 177 bottom; © Image Source/Getty Images: 68 top; © Global Book Publishing Pty. Ltd., 2003: 19 bottom, 20 bottom, 21 top, 64 second down, 65 top, 87 bottom, 174 top; © Saxon Holt/PhotoBotanic: 21 third down, 45, 207 top; © iStockphoto: Kiyoshi Takahase Segundo 16, Michael Kurtz 18, Greg Nicholas 22, Cheryl Meyer 28, Dave Logan 32, Merlin Farwell 34, Jeffrey Hochstrasser 37 right, Greg Nicholas 40 bottom, Anne Kitzman 41 bottom, Sherri Camp 42 right, Irena Ivanova 56, James Bowers 65 second down, 72 Marcel Pelletier, bowlinggranny 103 bottom, David Dolah 146, Anssi Ruuska 154, Judith Bicking 158, Vorakorn Tuvajitt 159, Milo Jokic 161 top, Sally Scott 177 top, Michael Blanc 194 bottom, Jonathan Cook 196, Emilio Chan 215 top, Gerry Tarney 215 bottom, Charles Humphries 228; © Rosemary Kautzky: 91, 93 bottom, 98 bottom right, 99 second down; © Christopher P. Lindsey: 208 second down; MACORE, Inc.: 46, 85 top, 86 top, 87 top, 98 second and third down, 104 middle, 138 bottom, 139 third down, 149 top right, 186 top, 187 bottom, 193 bottom; © Charles Mann: 162 top; © Photo courtesy of Mountain Valley Growers: 207 bottom; © New England Wildflower Society/Jean Baxter: 197 bottom. *NEWFS is America's oldest plant conservation institution and promotes the conservation of North American native plants. Located at Garden in the Woods, Framingham, MA. (www.newfs.org or 508-877-7630)*; © Judith Worley/Painet, Inc.: 175 third down, © Bill Beatty/Painet, Inc.: 176 bottom, © Rob Simpson/Painet Inc.: 198 bottom; © Jerry Pavia: 234 bottom right; Giles Prett/Storey Publishing: 36, 65 third down; © Sylvia Smith: 54 bottom, 139 second down; © Martin Wall: 64 top and bottom, 78, 139 top, 150 bottom, 175 bottom, 197 middle, 198 top, 207 middle, 208 bottom two; © Ellen Zachos: 3, 44, 68 bottom, 69 top, 70, 86 middle and bottom, 93 top, 97 bottom, 98 top and bottom left, 99 top, third down, and bottom, 102 left, 103 top, 105, 116, 117, 118, 125, 127, 128, 149 top left and bottom, 150 top and middle, 151 bottom, 152 top, 174 bottom, 176 second and third down, 177 middle, 192, 193 middle, 194 middle, 195 bottom, 201, 208 top, 219, 222, 232

Index

Page numbers in *italics* indicate photographs or illustrations. Page numbers in **bold** indicate tables.

Index continued

194, *194*
damping-off disease, 10
dandelion, 197, *197*
Datura metel (angel's trumpet), 93, 148
Daucus carota (Queen Anne's lace), 167, 176, *176*
Davallia fejeensis (squirrel's foot fern), 99, *99*
daylilies, *186*
day-neutral strawberries, 52, 53–54
dead trees, 75, 118–19, 132
decks
    container concerns, 46, 47, *48*, 57, 59
    See also terrace gardens
decomposition aids for compost, 217, 218
deer, 146–53
    deer-resistant plants, 138, 148–52, *149–52*, 153
Deervik, 153
depth of soil, 35, 38, 216
desiccation, 226
Diamond Frost (*Euphorbia* 'Diamond Frost'), 193, *193*
diffused light for photographs, 128–29
Digitalis purpurea (foxglove), **13**, 150, *150*
dinosaur gardens, 94–99, *95*, *97*
    plants, 97–99, *97–99*
direct sowing, 12
diseases, 10
    See also pests
dividing plants, *180, 182*, 185–89, *186*, *188–89*
    preparation, 187
    rhizomes, 186
    timing, 186, 187
    tools, 188, *188–89, 225, 225*
    tubers, 225, *225*
    See also transplanting
dogwood, red- or yellow-twig (*Cornus alba* cultivars), 177, *177*, 231
Dolichos lablab (hyacinth bean), 105, *105*
doll's-eyes (*Actaea pachypoda*), 149, *149*
dormant oil sprays, 171
drainage
    blueberries, 156
    containers, *47, 48*, 66, 92, 97, *134*
    materials for, *48*, 97
    raised beds, 35, 38
    See also overwatering
dried-out soil, watering, 32
drip irrigation, 58, 69, 124, *124*
drought-tolerant plants. *See* xeric plants
dry conditions
    antidesiccants, 226
    watering techniques, 31
    See also xeric plants; xeriscapes
dusty miller (*Centaurea cineraria* 'Colchester White'), 193, *193*
dwarf cattail (*Typha minima*), 85, *85*
dyes in mulch, 221

E

Echinacea purpurea (purple coneflower), **77**
Echinops ritro (globe thistle), 175, *175*
edible wild plants, 196–98, *197–98*
egg sprays to repel deer, 153
Eichhornia crassipes (water hyacinth), 87, *87*
elderflower, 108, *108*
    champagne, 106–10, *107*
elephant ear (*Colocasia esculenta*), 85, *85*
elephant ears (*Caladium* hybrid), 181, *181*, **184**, 193, *193*, 223, *223*
emetics for cats, 204, 208
Ensete ventricosum (ornamental banana), **184**
entertaining in gardens, 80, *80*, 235, *235*, 237, *237*
Epimedium species (barrenworts), 187, *187*
Equisetum species (horsetails), 86, *86*, 96, 98, *98*
Eryngium sp. (sea holly), *68*, **71**
Eupatorium purpureum (Joe-Pye weed), 176, *176*
Euphorbia 'Diamond Frost,' 193, *193*
evening gardens, 190–95, *191–95*
everbearing strawberries, 52, 53–54
evergreens, 230–31, *230–31*
extending seasons, 22–24, 35

F

fall
    bulb planting, 7, *7*, 224
    dividing, 186, 225, *225*
    garden assessment, 222
    harvesting, 206
    overwintering plants, 89, *89*, 181, 222–27, *223–27*
    transplanting, 223
false cypress (*Chamaecyparis obtusa*), **45**
family gardens, 236, 237
farmers, 210–13, *212–15*
feeders, 18, 19, 72–74, 78, 209
fences for deer, 152–53
Fenway Victory Gardens, *142*
fermenting Elderflower Champagne, 109, 110
ferns, 97–99, *97, 98, 99*
fertilizing, 153, 220
    as a deer repellent, 153
    grow-bags, 57
    hanging planters, 30, 31
    recycled containers, 93
    tropical plants, 182, *183*
    xeriscapes, 69
fescue, large blue (*Festuca amethystina*), **71**
Festuca amethystina (large blue fescue), **71**
fiberglass containers, 47
fiberglass tool handles, 41
field garlic, 197–98, *197*
fire extinguishers, 80
fire pits, 79–81, *80–81, 235*
    See also fireplaces
fireplaces as containers, 69
    See also fire pits

fires, 80
firethorn (*Pyracantha coccinea*), 177, *177*
Fittonia verschaffeltii (mosaic plant), **184**
flash-banging noisemakers, 119–20, *119*
flats, 10, *14–15, 15*
flat stones, 162, *162*
floating plants, 88
flower gardens. *See* cutting gardens
flowering maples (*Abutilon* hybrids), **184**
flowering tobacco (*Nicotiana sylvestris*), 194, *194*
fluorescents, compact, 201, 203, **203**
fluorescent tubes, 201, *201*, **203**
foliage vines, 102–3, *102–3*
food
    CSAs, 210–15, *212–15*
    food bank gardens, 144
    See also berries (edible); foraging; recipes
food banks, 144
foraging among wild plants, 196–98, *197–98*
forcing bulbs, 2–6, *5*, **6**
forks, 189, *189*
forsythia (*Forsythia* species and hybrids), 174, *174*
Forsythia species and hybrids, 174, *174*
fountains, 89, 209
foxglove (*Digitalis purpurea*), **13**, 150, *150*
fragrant plants, 136, 139, *139*, 153, 190–92, 195, *195*, 207, *207*
frames for raised beds, 36–37
framing shots, 126–27
frost dates, 23
frost protection, 22–24, 45–46, 92
    containers, 45–46, *47*, 92, 227, 230
    See also overwintering plants
Fuchsia hybrids and species, 20, *20*
fuchsias (*Fuchsia* hybrids and species), 20, *20*
full moon maple (*Acer palmatum*), **45**
fungal activity in soil, 156
fungi, damping-off disease, 10
furniture for gardens, 234–36, *234*
fuzzy-leaved plants, 136–39, *137–38*, 152

G

Gaillardia x *grandiflora* (blanketflower), **77**
games in gardens, 237
gardener's hotline, 52
garden forks, 189, *189*
garden furniture, 234–36, *234*
garden locations, 25–27, 132, 134
    cat gardens, 209
    community gardens, 142
    hardiness zones, 26–27, *238*
    heat zones, 27
    microclimates, *27*, 45–46
    raised bed sites, 38
    soil depth, 35, 38, 216
garlic, field, 197–98, *197*
geophytes, 223–24, *223*
    See also bulbs; rhizomes; tubers

Index continued

245

Index continued

rhubarb (*Rheum rhabarbarum*), 152, *152*
ribbon bush (*Homalocladium platycladum*), **184**
Ricinus communis 'Carmencita' (castor bean), 181, **184**
rock. *See* stone; stones
rocky soil, 34, 39–40, *40*
rooftop gardens, *57*
  container weight, 46, 47, 48, 57, 59
  irrigation, 58
  as microclimates, *27*, 45–46
  See also terrace gardens
rose hips, 231
rosemary (*Rosmarinus officinalis*), 65, *65*, 139, *139*
roses (watering can spouts), 11
Rosmarinus officinalis (rosemary), 65, *65*, 139, *139*
row markers for seeds, *11*, 15
rubber tool handles, *41*, 42
Rudbeckia species and hybrids (black-eyed Susan), **77**, 111, 224
Rushing, Felder, 119
ryegrass (*Lolium* species), 208

S
safety
  fires, 80
  foraging, 196–98
  insecticides, 18, 78
  poisonous plants, 148
  slug repellents, 169
  soil contaminants, 144
  stone handling, 163
  tool use, 42, 188
sage, 65, *65*
  clary (*Salvia sclarea*), 138, *138*
Sagina subulata (Irish moss), 98, *98*
sago palm (*Cycas revoluta*), 99, *99*
Salvia sclarea (clary sage), 138, *138*
Salvia species (sage), 65, *65*
sand cherry, purple-leaf (*Prunus cistena*), **71**
sandy soil, 217
Sansevieria species and hybrids (snake plants), **184**, 202
Santolina chamaecyparissus, 139, *139*
santolina (*Santolina chamaecyparissus*), 139, *139*
Scabiosa caucasica (pincushion flower), **77**
scale, 169, *169*
scarecrows, 116–20, *117–19*
scarlet runner beans (*Phaseolus coccineus*), 105, *105*
scented geraniums (*Pelargoniaum* species), 139, *139*
scented plants, 136, 139, *139*, 153, 190–92, 207, *207*
scillas, **6**
sea holly (*Eryngium* sp.), 68, **71**
seasonal eating, 213–14
seasonal plant changes, 30
  See also fall; winter

season extension, 22–24, 35
Sedum 'Autumn Joy,' 69, *69*, 224
Sedum seiboldii (stonecrop), 69, *69*, 139, *139*
seed flats, 10, *14–15*, 15
seedlings
  cold frames, 23–24
  cotyledons, 12, *12*
  damping-off disease, 10
  frost protection, 22–24
  hardening off, 12–13, 24
  planting, 13, *62*
  thinning, 12, *63*
  transplanting, 12–13, *13*, 22–23, 188
  See also young plants
seeds, 8–13, *9*, *11*, *14–15*, **13**
  bird gardens, 76
  container choices, 10
  cost, 9–10
  germinating, 10–11, **13**
  growth process, 12, *12*
  large, 15
  light, 10–11, 15, **13**, 201, *201*, **203**
  row markers, *11*, 15
  soil mixes, 10
  watering, 11, 15, *15*, 12
  See also seedlings
Selaginella kraussiana (little club moss), 98, *98*
Selaginella uncinata (peacock moss), **184**
Sempervivum tectorum (hens and chicks), 69, *69*, **71**
senses, gardens for, 136–39, *138–39*
serviceberries (*Amelanchier* species), **45**, **77**
shadblow (*Amelanchier* species), **45**
shade, 26
  for cats, 209
  plants for, 20, *20*, 104, *104*, **184**
  water gardens, 84
  xeriscaping tips, 68
shovels, 40–41, *43*
shrubs
  bottle trees, 118–19, *118*
  frost protection, 227
  See also shrubs by name
Silene laciniata (Mexican catchfly), 21, *21*
silver vine (*Actinidia polygama*), 208, *208*
sites for gardens, 25–27, 38
six-packs, planting, *63*
size
  container trees vs. in ground, 45
  tropical plants, 180, 182, **184**
  See also sizing
sizing
  containers, 45
  fire pits, 81
  water garden plants, 84
  See also size
slugs, 169, *169*

snake plants (*Sansevieria* species and hybrids), **184**, 202
snow, plant damage from, 227
soaker hose, 123, *123*
soap, insecticidal, 170, 171
soil, 216–21
  alkaline, 219
  amending, 39–40, 69, 156, *183*, 219–21, *220*
  cat recreation areas, 209
  clay, 217
  compaction, 35
  containers, 47, 62, 92
  depth, 35, 38, 216
  fungal activity, 156
  hydrogels in, 31, 70
  loamy, 217
  macronutrients, 219–20
  nematodes (beneficial), 166
  mixtures, 217
  pH, 156, 218–19
  potting mix, 10, 30–31, 70, 92, 132, *134*
  preparing, 14
  raised beds, 35
  rocky, 34, 39–40, *40*
  safety checks, 144
  sandy, 217
  seed starts, 10
  strawberries, 53
  tilth, 217
  weight, 47, 48, 59, 62, 92, 97
  See also compost
Solanostemon scutellariodes (coleus), **184**
Solanum pyracanthum, 138, *138*, **184**
solanum (*Solanum pyracanthum*), 138, *138*, **184**
solstice celebrations, 80
sorbet, strawberry, 50, 55
Sorbus species (mountain ash), **77**
spades, 40–41, *40*, 188
spider mites, 171
Spirea thunbergii (yellow spirea), **71**
spirea, yellow (*Spirea thunbergii*), **71**
spittle bugs, 169–70
sprays
  antidesiccants, 226
  bug repellents, 170, 171
  deer repellents, 153
  fertilizers, 220
  See also insecticides
spring bulbs, 2–7, *3–6*, 224
spruce branches, 231
squirrel's foot fern (*Davallia fejeensis*), 99, *99*
Stachys byzantina (lamb's ear), 138, *138*
staking plants, 111–18, *112–15*, *115*
standing stones, 163, *163*
stonecrop (*Sedum seiboldii*), 69, *69*, 139, *139*
stone fire pits, 79–81, *80–81*, *235*